Fragile Delivery:

Operation Babylift C 5-A Galaxy Crash

By
Surviving Crew Member
Phillip R. Wise

ISBN-10: 147506909X
ISBN-13: 9781475069099

To Sufriana,
My Jewel on Earth

FOREWORD

I sat at the Ft. Myers Florida airport waiting to board my flight back home following a presentation I'd just given at Hammond Field celebrating the 30th anniversary of the erection of the Vietnam Veterans Memorial Wall. A woman came and sat across from me and immersed herself in a book. Her husband joined her a few minutes later and immediately noticed the model C-5A Galaxy aircraft I had placed on the table next to me. "Is that an award or a gift," the middle-aged man asked. "It's a little bit of both," I answered, and began to explain why I was carrying the model.

The organizers of the event at Hammond Field had invited me and other veterans of Operation Babylift and relatives to participate and read the names of the people who lost their lives on the C-5A Galaxy crash that occurred on April 4, 1975, to keep their memory alive.

We presented The Heather Constance Noone Memorial Plaque to the Traveling Vietnam Veterans Memorial Wall and Museum. The guests in our group included Lana Noone (the plaque was in honor of her late daughter), Vicki Curtiss Fernandez, Ann Vermeire, Ed Gosselin, and me.

At first I was reluctant tell the story of the significance of the model aircraft because my flight would soon board. I could see that the man was thoroughly interested in the model, while his wife remained glued to her book. I decided to briefly tell him my story.

I began by saying the model aircraft was given to me by a young man name Daniel Bischoff who survived an airplane crash during Operation Babylift during the fall of Saigon, South Vietnam, on April 4, 1975, when he was a baby. Suddenly, the woman stopped reading her book and focused intently on what I had to say.

As I got deeper and deeper into my story, the couple leaned closer and closer to me. I noticed myself getting a little choked up at the same time they did. Before I realized it, time had flown by and the PA announced final boarding for my flight. I had to leave but the couple yearned for more. Before I left I gave them my web site address with my contact information.

When I arrived home I received an e-mail from the couple inviting me to speak at their church. It warmed my heart to know that my story had touched them so much. It made me realize that maybe others would love to hear such a miraculous story, too.

***

My name is Phillip Romon Wise. I was born on March 11, 1952 in Hanford, California and again on April 4, 1975, in South Vietnam. I know exactly what you are thinking. How can a person have two birthdays? On April 4, 1975, I was involved in a horrific plane crash on the outskirts of Saigon, South Vietnam. My second birthday occurred when I awakened from two days of unconsciousness in the intensive care unit at Clark Air Force Base hospital in the Philippines.

Imagine waking up and having absolutely no idea where you are, only to have that thought superseded by searing pain racing through your, stiff, bruised body. That is precisely where I found myself. Obviously, something had gone terribly wrong. I was in critical condition and I had no idea how I got those injuries. All I really knew about the early moments of my second birth was that I was alive; barely alive but alive nonetheless. And, I knew at that moment that in God's world as long as you have breath in your body, the possibilities of what you can accomplish are endless.

Despite the uncertainty, I knew I must have been lucky to have survived whatever happened to me. It didn't take me long to figure out that our plane had crashed. Moreover, when I learned the full details of the terrible circumstances that put me in that hospital bed, thousands of miles away from my hometown of Flint, Michigan, I no longer considered myself lucky. I considered myself blessed.

As an Aero Medical Evacuation Technician in the United States Air Force, I participated in Operation Babylift: The mass evacuation of orphans out of Saigon, South Vietnam during the final days of the Vietnam War. President Gerald R. Ford ordered the military to evacuate thousands of children, many of whom were infants. They were to be taken out of harm's way as the bloody war entered its final stage. Some of the children had lost both parents in the war. Others, fathered by American soldiers, were simply abandoned, unwanted and scorned. Yet more were sent away by their families in hopes of finding a better life in a better place.

I always thought what a heart-wrenching decision it must have been for those families, the mothers and fathers, to give their children away. I am sure they felt great angst, and even guilt. However, it's really an incredible act of love to get a child out of a dire situation in hopes that child will have a better life.

Undoubtedly, many of those children would have faced a hard, difficult life, or maybe even been killed, if they had remained in Vietnam. They certainly deserved a chance at a better life. They were just children, sweet and innocent, God's gift to the world, who unfortunately found themselves in deadly circumstances.

The children of Vietnam were the true casualties of war. It was our job to get those babies out of harm's way, and we took on that responsibility with an extra sense of pride, knowing our orders came directly from the President of the United States. In the end, more than 2,000 babies were evacuated during Operation Babylift, and given a chance at a new life. And, although I nearly died from the injuries I suffered, the entire experience made me a better person, and gave me a greater appreciation of life. And that is why I note two birthdays.

Only a miracle helped me survive that crash. Almost 40 years later, I still cannot give a reason why I survived, while so many others did not. In fact, I have often wondered why I survived. Did I grab that cargo tie-down strap, or did I grab something else? Did something cushion the blow of the impact? Was I thrown about the aircraft and somehow my limbs got trapped in the wired cables as the aircraft broke apart? My left leg injury may give credence to such a theory. Because I was unconscious, I just do not know, and probably will never know fully what happened during those frantic moments.

I have even thought about undergoing hypnosis to get that day back, and perhaps find out what really happened. As for now, I have concluded God had more in store for me. When I think about all the lives I have touched by sharing my story after so many years of being afraid to discuss the tragedy, I feel rewarded. It took nine years after the crash for me to be able to talk about what happened during that life altering incident. In those days, opponents of the war painted Vietnam Veterans in a negative light, often calling us "baby killers." Most people did not know my story and had no idea I had suffered severe injuries as a result of trying to save babies. War is hell and so many have suffered.

WRECKAGE OF THE C5-A GALAXY APRIL 1975
(Courtesy of Larry Engelmann)

PROLOGUE

I have a dream, a recurring dream. I'm standing on a platform 25,000 feet in the air. I'm looking down and all I can see is the cloud cover. I'm not sure how I got here. Not sure how to get back to my bed. Not sure how to get back to my life. Not sure what I'm going to do. And before I can think about it for one more second I step off. And down I go. I'm flying!

I had often dreamed of flying. Towel around my neck. Hands out. Wind coming up to meet my face as I step off Momma's couch -- and for just those brief seconds before the coffee table catches the side of my head and breaks my fall and I roll over and laugh and laugh and laugh – I am flying, even if for just one second.

Only now the seconds are turning into minutes and down I fall. I'm engulfed by other kids swirling around and around. Never seen any kids like this before. But they are falling, too. Only they aren't laughing. They are crying and screaming and I grab one by the hand as I float by and help calm another with just a touch on his shoulder. And I say, "It's gonna be okay."

But now I'm really flying. Through the cloud cover and I'm picking up speed. I reach to adjust my mask. But I don't have one. I fumble for the rip cord but I don't have one of those either. The wind whips with such strength I can barely make out the ground coming up to meet me. I close my eyes. I don't want to be in this dream any more. I don't want to keep falling. I don't want to crash. I want to live.

And that was that. I hit the earth. And I roll over and over and over and over like I used to do on that hill over by Clifford Street when I was 9 years old. I would just roll and roll and then end up flat on my back.

I am in my bed. I am safe. Covers pulled up just right. Just up to the tip of my chin. I can hear Momma's voice and Daddy patting his foot to the radio in the kitchen. And I know I am gonna be all right. I sigh a very deep sigh of relief. I am home. In my bed. Nothing could get me now. I really am safe. But I'm not. I am still falling from 25,000 feet in the air. Oh no! Is this a dream?

JOURNAL ENTRY
JANUARY 1975

- *The New Year is here, January 1975, and I am assigned to the 9th Aero Medical Evacuation Group (AEG) and into my second year on tour at Clark Air Base, Republic of the Philippines. At the 9th AEG our mission is to airlift military personnel, patients and passengers to and from a number of military bases throughout Southeast Asia. Clark Air Base has the region's largest hospital and has the staff to accommodate almost any type of injury or surgery.*
- *The 374th Military Airlift Wing is under Pacific Air Command, Headquarters Hickham Air Force Base, Hawaii. The 9th AEG is operating under the 374th MAW, and maintains four DC-9 nightingale aircrafts. They are positioned on the tarmac ready for aero medical evacuation missions servicing all of Southeast Asia.*
- *The 9th Aero Medical Evacuation Group is where medical evacuation missions are generated. Our control center maintains our crew availability roster and is where pre-flight planning takes place. When battlefield casualties occur the call comes into the control center and a crew is assembled. The urgency of the mission determines how soon we are airborne. If the mission is a scheduled one, we operate on a set time table. But, if the mission is urgent we have to be airborne within an hour.*

CHAPTER ONE

I am the son of Roosevelt Wise, Jr. and Minnie Zell Jackson Wise Vincent, of Pine Bluff, Ark. I am an African-American. It is important to explain my ethnicity because the mere color of my, and my ancestor's skin, greatly shaped the life experiences of my family. If you were black in the South during the 1930s, '40s, '50s, and '60s, the color of your skin made a tremendous difference in everything you did.

It determined where you lived, worked, went to school, traveled, attended church, and what hospital would accept you. The color of your skin even determined where you were buried when you died. In those days, blacks were nothing more than second-class citizens in the eyes of most people. My mother lived on the East Side of town, in an all-black segregated section of Pine Bluff. Dad grew up in another segregated area called the Brickyard. People regarded the 'Bricks' as a nicer area for blacks; and teachers, lawyers, doctors and businesspersons lived there.

The name Brickyard came from that fact that the roads were paved in brick and many of the homes were made from brick. A brick home signaled that a family had a good income. Despite the racism of the time, blacks found a way to carry themselves with great dignity, regardless of the circumstances confronting them.

My mother always told us stories of those days and the struggles that black folk had to deal with. We took pride in her defiance. "I would rather walk downtown than sit on the back of one of those buses," she would say. And that is exactly what she and a lot of other black folk did. Many a day she walked from our house three miles to get to town. I think about all those people who lived in those conditions, and I wonder how they must feel to see the same country that once demoted them to the back of a bus elect a black president.

As a teenager, mother had a best friend, Gladis, who lived in the Brickyard. She would go over to Gladis' house to visit. During one such visit Gladis introduced my mother to her friend Roosevelt. My future mother and father connected immediately, beyond friendship, much to the chagrin of Gladis. He fell for my mother from the moment he laid eyes on her. The love at first sight thing must run in the family. Many years later I would experience that very same kind of love when I first laid eyes on Tessie, the woman who would become my wife. But that's getting ahead of the story.

For a while it looked like my parents wouldn't get together. Initially, their relationship got put on hold because mom left Pine Bluff, with her cousin, to go live with her aunt Florence in New Jersey. Mother left for New Jersey in the mid-40s, but she returned a few years later when her mother, my grandmother Carrie Jackson, became ill. My mother, a dutiful daughter, came back to Pine Bluff with her two children Pamela and Cedric. She and dad began dating again and dated for about year, until Grandma Carrie died. When Grandma Carrie passed on, my mother decided to move to California to live with her aunt Sally.

But this time, Roosevelt Wise Jr., a very smart and determined young man, followed her. He was not going to let her get away again. Dad worked at a hotel in Los Angeles, and made the two-hour ride north to Hanford and visited mom whenever he could. They married in 1952, and eventually had four children, with Felecia, Rickie and Kerwin following me. It's funny how fate brings people together. What if dad had preferred Gladis instead of mom? What if mom never moved back to Arkansas from New Jersey?

As I have learned in my amazing journey through life, a lot of things have to fall perfectly in place for other things to come to fruition. Fortunately for me, the stars aligned with my parents, and they got together and built a family. In 1956, when I was 4 years old, we left California for Michigan. Dad got a job working in a chemical plant in Detroit. Not long after, he got a job in Flint, Michigan, about 70 miles north of Detroit. Flint was a booming mid-sized city famous for being the birthplace of General Motors, and a major producer of GM vehicles. People called it Buick City.

Although dad moved to Michigan from California after living in Arkansas, indirectly he was part of the great migration of blacks to the North from the South, where Jim Crow laws and blatant racism made it nearly impossible for black families to prosper. During that time, 'up North' was viewed as the promise land by blacks. It's easy to see why. Not only did racism hold people down, but there were no quality jobs for blacks in the Mississippi Delta, or plains of Alabama, Georgia and Arkansas.

However, the steel mills of Gary, Indiana, the booming metropolis of Chicago, and Detroit, home of America's auto industry, along with Flint, offered blacks a chance to earn a decent living. The GM plants in Flint hired blacks in well-paying jobs with benefits and union backing. And while the work was often grueling, those jobs laid the foundation for Black America's middle class.

And while racism certainly existed in those Northern cities, it wasn't nearly as bad as in the South. When we moved from Detroit to Flint, we lived with my father's sister, Aunt Edna. I was only 4 at the time, and really don't remember much. We lived there for about a year, and then we moved from Aunt Edna's and made a brief stay on a street named Floral Park on the Southside.

I vividly remember living on Floral Park, because that's when my dad sliced his hand trying to cut a limb off a pear tree in our backyard with a knife. My oldest brother and I were about to get a spanking because we went next door without permission after being warned not to, over and over again. In the process of hacking the limb, Dad severely cut his hand and we were frightened because his thumb was bleeding profusely. But, at the same time we were relieved that the punishment was on hold. We hoped that he would forget the spanking; unfortunately he didn't forget.

While my Dad's hand was healing, he was neatly braiding an ironing cord he took off an old iron. He used black electrical tape to braid that cord. Two weeks had passed and my brother and I wondered what he was up to. Boy, were we in for a surprise! That braided ironing cord turned out to be a tailor-made belt that he patiently designed for us. My brother and I got a whipping that I remember vividly to this day. We lost that designer belt quickly. It's funny today but not so back then.

We lived in an apartment building on the top floor. Our family also grew by two, with the births of Kerwin and Darrell. The one memory I have from that period is the Beecher Tornado that practically destroyed the community just north of Flint. The Beecher tornado killed 116 people and injured hundreds of others, while destroying 360 homes. Although we were on the south side of town, five or so miles away from Beecher, we were hit with a torrential downpour and wind gusts that caused severe flooding on our street.

We really began to settle into Flint when we moved to 1807 Clifford Street. I was about 9 years old. And because we had five boys in our family, our house quickly became the center of activity on the block. My father was very strict about watching where we played, so we didn't wander too far. Instead, kids started coming over to our house to play. We played year-round winter, spring, summer and fall. Back then we got mountains of snow in brutal winters every year. We played football in the snow and I made lots of money shoveling snow throughout the neighborhoods. My parents were always proud of me for wanting to work.

I got my work ethic from my dad. Dad was the bread-winner. He worked long and hard for General Motors for 36-years and only missed five days of work. While Dad was at work, Mom was at home with the kids. She was a nurturer who would read to us daily and always looked to stimulate our minds. In addition, she taught us early about the importance of responsibility. My brothers, sisters, and I were assigned weekly chores. And in order for us to experience a variety of tasks, my mother would rotate our schedule every week. Our responsibilities included washing clothes, mopping floors and washing dishes. I don't know of many kids who liked doing chores, however, those assignments taught us a lot about responsibility. My mother and father showed us what a day's work meant, not just in terms of earning a dollar, but fulfilling responsibility as a person.

Even with the chores, I had great fun growing up with my siblings. My eldest sister Pam would often pay me to do her chores, which I would do happily. I was about 7 or 8 years old at the time, and I can say that was the beginning of my career as a young entrepreneur. Dad did not give us a big allowance. The quarter he would give us would be enough to go skating, but that was about it. I soon realized that was not enough, so I had to go out and get some other funds. That's how I got into doing other jobs.

My first job was as a delivery boy of the Michigan Chronicle, a black newspaper that covered the events that affected the African-American community. Black newspapers talked about issues of the community that the mainstream papers didn't. I felt a lot of responsibility on my shoulders to make sure people got their latest editions in a timely manner. The weekly paper had a unique color – green -- not the typical white color of a newspaper. I have no idea why they decided to have a green newspaper. But it was my job to deliver it throughout the neighborhood, and that's what I did. In fact, my brother older brother Cedric and I threw the newspapers so well, we were featured in the paper as carriers of the week.

A few years later, I worked for Mendell Vaughn, who was the community director at Clark Elementary School. During those days every school in Flint had a community director who operated after-school programs for kids. They supervised a variety of programs that were open to anyone in the community. It was a great deal because we always had a safe place to go and positive things to do. Wednesday became my favorite day because it was Skate Night. Mr. Vaughn gave me the job of renting out skates and repairing them. I was in the fifth grade, which made me about 11 years old. After skating ended, I also cleaned the floor. Whatever my task was, I tried to do it to the best of my abilities. I felt a strong sense of pride by having a job.

But, without question, my favorite duty was re-stocking the soda machine. Why? Mr. Vaughn would always give me a free ice-cold soda. My soda of choice was a 7-Up. I loved 7-Up, especially ice cold, which seemed to go down better. Now, I had two jobs because I did yard work for our neighbor; so I decided to hire my brother, Rickie, to do my chores at home. It was a decision I needed to make for my burgeoning business empire. Friday was a big night for me and it was also chore day. With Rickie doing my chores, I had time to go skating and do my homework for school.

Under Mr. Vaughn's encouragement, I was a dedicated flag boy in fourth grade and a crossing guard in fifth grade and never received a demerit. Mr. Vaughn had a tremendous influence on me; he helped shape the person I am today. He gave me a job and responsibility, and he showed me what it takes to be a leader.

Mr. Vaughn taught me everything from how to do a proper sit-up to how to operate and manage a business. He appointed me 'captain', which meant I was a person he could count on. That meant a lot to me and did wonders for my self esteem. I became a confident young man.

Mr. Vaughn always provided positive activities for the young people, such as kickball, softball, basketball, football, and pom-pom-tackle. Pom-pom-tackle, a game we played on a large dirt/grassy field, was sort of like football. One had to run from one end of the field to the other end without getting tackled. It was a free-for-all rumble, which means anyone could tackle you once you began your run. Needless to say, it was extremely difficult to run from one end of the field to the other end without getting tackled. It was mostly a game we played during recess at school. When the recess bell rang we returned to class noticeably dirty, sweaty and often bruised and bleeding.

Sadly, Mr. Vaughn passed away from the injuries he suffered after breaking up a fight with one of the neighborhood rivals. Someone threw a skate during the brawl and, somehow, the skate gashed Mr. Vaughn in the side of his neck, seriously injuring him. Although he survived, when Mr. Vaughn finally returned to work at my elementary school, he never was the same. He just couldn't find the strength and energy that he once had. I will always be grateful to him. And looking back, I realize today how lucky we were as kids to have those kinds of programs in place. When Mr. Vaughn eventually succumbed to his injury, it was a sad day for me.

PHILLIP R. WISE AT 6 MONTHS OLD

CHAPTER TWO

The doorbell rang, followed by a strong powerful knock at my door. My wife answered and called me up from downstairs where I was playing pool. At the door stood a huge man dressed in a suit with a shirt and tie.

"Mr. Phillip R. Wise?"

"Who's asking?" I replied. He gave me his name and said he was a private investigator hired to locate me.

"Who hired you?"

He left without answering or saying another word.

A day or so later, in January 1984, I got a phone call from a producer at the ABC News show 20/20 inviting me to come to Washington, DC to do an interview at the Vietnam Veterans Memorial Wall. They had learned that I had been in the Operation Babylift C-5A Galaxy crash. I accepted their invitation and they made all the travel arrangements for me.

This was big news and I shared it with my wife and family right away. I had never talked much about my Operation Babylift experience. My parents and siblings never asked about what happened to me. They thought the airplane crash had been minor because I looked normal when I came home in the spring of 1976 with the exception of having to use a walking cane. My facial scars were well healed. Before I left the Air Force I had scar revision on my face to reduce the keloids that had become very noticeable. I wore clothes that covered my arms and legs. So most of my family, other than my wife, had no clue what Operation Babylift was all about and what had happened to me.

I flew to Washington, DC and stayed in a hotel in Georgetown. I had never stayed in such a fabulous hotel before; it must have been at least a five-star hotel. One of the producers, Danny Schechter, came to my room to interview me. Danny was very nice and extremely knowledgeable about Operation Babylift. He had done a lot of research on the Babylift and my interview was one of many that contributed to his investigation.

The 20/20 interview aired on April 4, 1984, nine years after the crash of the C-5A Galaxy airplane. ABC News correspondent Tom Jarriel did my interview. Barbara Walters and Hugh Downs anchored the 20/20 show from ABC News headquarters in New York. Tom and I walked down the mall corridor at the Vietnam Veterans Memorial Wall as I shared my story with him. The camera crew followed us and I came to a place on the wall where I saw my fallen crew members' names. Their names were placed on the wall under the year 1975; all soldiers' names on the wall are placed under the year they died in Vietnam.

I read the names of all my crew members and gave a brief description of their job title. Reading my crew members' names had me feeling a little emotional. I began to choke up and had to gather myself. We continued to talk and I knelt down where my crew member names were, and told Tom Jarriel: "This is where my name would have been had I not survived the crash."

I felt sad during that interview, and I felt a little guilty when seeing all those names on the wall. Each name had a family, a brother, a sister, a father, a mother, a daughter or a son.

The day the show aired was the first time my family had ever seen the wreckage of the C-5A Galaxy crash site. They were stunned. They had no idea that I had gone through such a tragic ordeal. My telephone went off like never before once the show aired.

Phillip's parents
ROOSEVELT
WISE JR. and
MINNIE WISE

PHIL WITH SIBLINGS: PAMELA, CEDRIC, PHILLIP, FELECIA,
RICKIE, AND KERWIN

JOURNAL ENTRY
FIRST WEEK JANUARY 1975

- *Following New Year's Day, I know I have to fly on a mission to Yokota AB Japan, but I have to settle into my new apartment before leaving. The trip is scheduled for Tuesday and my girlfriend, Tessie, wants me to go to the furniture store with her before leaving on my trip. Tessie is a beautiful, tall, young Filipino girl. She makes sure that I take care of business before leaving on a trip because she knows it is very likely that I may not come home as scheduled. I often stay longer on some missions.*

- *Monday is here and I decide to crash at the barracks (Building 6468 room 122) over night. This is something I often do when scheduled to fly the following morning. I leave my apartment and head to checkpoint. Checkpoint is the main gate at Clark Air Base. The mode of transportation for local Filipinos is jeepneys, tricycles, and calisas. My apartment is near Gen. MacArthur highway and I walk there and ride a jeepney to checkpoint. A jeepney is an old WWII jeep converted into a taxi that holds about 10 people. The time is about 2300 hours (11:00 pm) and I am standing waiting on a jeepney. I jump in the vacant seat up front on a jeepney full of passengers, sandwiching the lady in the middle, and put my left arm around the seat to try and get comfortable.*

- *I am wearing a nice looking gold watch and my arm is stretched across the front seat as we roll down MacArthur highway. Suddenly, I feel somebody pulling on my watch. I react by snatching my arm instantly and looking at my wrist. The watch is gone and so is the perpetrator. It is late and close to curfew so I just ride that jeepney to checkpoint.*

- *The base provides shuttle bus service throughout the entire base. I ride the shuttle bus to my barracks upset about what had just happened. As the bus rides around the base dropping passengers off, I am dozing off to sleep and waking up at each stop.*

- *Finally, I reach my stop and make it to my room and find my glossy shoes placed outside my door. Eddy, my houseboy, that's what the local employees who work in the barracks are called, shines my shoes, cleans my room and does my laundry for only seven dollars a week. I put my clothes away, double check my flight gear making sure I have everything. I say my prayers and go to bed.*

- *A lot of Americans are not aware that US Marines are fighting well after the pull out of Vietnam. They are stationed at a base in Thailand that boarders Laos and Cambodia. Many weapons are coming into Vietnam via Cambodia and Laos; our Marines are there to stop the flow of weapons. There are times when our Marines incur injuries and have to be evacuated.*

- *Officially we are not in Cambodia or Laos, but secret missions are launched into that country to engage the enemies. Unfortunately some of our Marines are injured and have to be airlifted out. That's where we come in, aerovac. Our DC-9 Nightingale lands at a base in Thailand near the border. The patient is transported by way of ambulance to be evacuated. These missions are priority or urgent missions and those patients have to be evacuated immediately. When on alert duty it is not uncommon to fly an urgent mission to Thailand to pick up one patient and fly right back to Clark AB. Clark is the closest medical facility equipped to treat a wide range of injuries.*

CHAPTER THREE

Finally, after a long wait inside the squadron the mission was on the way. It was early April and I had been alerted to fly at 0655 hours by the CQ (charge of quarters), five minutes before my duty was over. My initial thought was that maybe there was a mistake. I called the squadron to confirm the mission and was told that it was a go. I grabbed my bags and caught a taxi to the flight line. I ran toward the aircraft, a DC-9 Nightingale with the engines started and ready to taxi.

At this point I'm thinking that they were leaving without me. I waved my hand while running toward the aircraft trying to get them to stop. The aircraft stopped and the forward door opened. The flight engineer stepped out and asked "What can I do for you?"

I said, "I've been alerted to fly and I should be on the flight with you."

The flight engineer said, "This is just a training mission, we're going up and turning around and coming back."

I was baffled. I went inside the squadron office to find out what was going on and found TSgt. Turner Smith in the control center. "What's going on?" I asked. "Just hold tight Sgt. Wise," he said, and that's what I did for quite a long time. In fact, I was still waiting hours past 0700 hours, which was my off-duty time. But it didn't matter. I had my orders.

By 1000 hours, we were assembled in a briefing room, the flight crew and the medical crews. The wing commander and our squadron commander led the briefing. We learned that the fall of Saigon, Vietnam was imminent. Yet thousands of people were fleeing to Saigon from the north, including many orphans displaced from orphanages, hoping to get out of Vietnam from there. The commanders estimated that unknown numbers of Amer-Asian kids were trapped in Saigon and the fear was that they would be treated badly, persecuted or killed if left behind.

We were told that President Gerald R. Ford had ordered Operation Babylift. The US government set up a $2 million fund to evacuate more than 2,500 Amer-Asian orphans from Vietnam. Even children who had parents were being given to orphanages in hopes of getting them out of Vietnam. We all were stunned in the briefing with the realization that the fall of South Vietnam had begun. We realized that this was a history-making event. And we were part of it.

The big surprise for the medical crew was that we would not use the C-141 or DC-9 Nightingale that we normally used, but instead we would be using the huge, five-story C-5A Galaxy. It would be the first time a C-5A Galaxy was used for an aerovac mission. The flight crew gave us a quick walk through of the C-5A Galaxy. I was amazed at the size of the aircraft. I stood there in awe of its massive doors and ramp. The belly had howitzers strapped down for delivery to Vietnam. We strategized with the flight crew and figured out what we needed to take for the kids. We took medicine, blankets, milk, water, diapers and anything we could think of that those babies might need.

We boarded the aircraft and took off for Tan Son Nhut Air Base, South Vietnam. Our medical team rode in the flight deck with the flight crew. We talked about what was happening in Vietnam, how the President would meet the C-5A Galaxy at Travis AFB California on its return to welcome the orphans to America. We were excited, thrilled. We talked about what to expect once we got to Vietnam. We wondered what condition the babies would be in, what the security situation would be like, and if the flight line would be shelled, or maybe the flight line would be overrun by refugees trying to escape the ensuing communist regime.

The medical team leaving Clark AB Philippines consisted of two nurses and four medical technicians. The nurses were 1st Lt. Marcie Wirtz Tate and 1st Lt. Harriet Goffinet Neill. The medical technicians were SMSgt. Olen H. Boutwell, TSgt. Denning C. Johnson, Sgt. Gregory B. Gemerik and I, Sgt. Phillip R. Wise. We were all from the 9th Aero Medical Evacuation Group, Clark AB Philippines. I was the senior medical technician with responsibility of assigning the other medical technicians to perform duties in different sections of the aircraft.

Marcie was MCD (Medical Crew Director) and Harriet served as the second nurse. Our assignment changed when we arrived in Saigon. The C-141 medical crew merged with us. Capt. Mary Klinker and Lt. Regina Aune were the flight nurses from the 10th Aerovac at Travis AB California. SSgt. James A. Hadley and SSgt. Michael G. Paget were the medical technicians. Once our crews merged, I remained the senior medical technician and Regina became the MCD. The Medical Crew Director, in charge of the medical team, worked as the second nurse and managed the medicine kit.

When our C-5A Galaxy crew landed at Ton Son Nhut, we taxied to an isolated area of the flight line. The doors opened and a gust of hot air rushed through the cabin. I looked out the huge cargo doors and saw a long line of buses parked on the tarmac. Heat waves misted around the buses. I thought, "I hope those buses are air conditioned," but I found out later that they weren't. Our medical crews got together and devised our assignments to work in the different sections of the aircraft. Regina Aune, Mary Klinker, DC Johnson, Michael Paget and I worked the cargo section. Marcie Wirtz, Harriet Goffinet, James Hadley, Greg Gemerik and Olen Boutwell worked the troop compartment upstairs.

We got our teams in place and were ready for enplaning the kids. We formed a chain line up to the troop compartment where we passed each child upstairs. They were placed two per seat in the approximately 77 seats upstairs. Downstairs we prepared the cargo section by placing military blankets throughout the cargo floor. The older kids were positioned downstairs. Some sat on the cat walk and the others sat on the floor. We used cargo tie down straps across our laps to secure us for takeoff. Normally loading passengers downstairs without seats was against Air Force regulation. An exception was made for this emergency evacuation mission to accommodate more people – so many that we did not have a manifest that accounted for everyone.

The powerful doors and the huge ramp closed, and we could hear the loud hydraulics as we prepared for takeoff. The door latches locked, the cargo cabin got dim and the cabin began to finally cool off after a long wait in the unbearable heat. My uniform was soaking wet from perspiration and I welcomed that cold air. The kids began to quiet down as the cabin cooled off. The C-5A Galaxy took off and we were airborne.

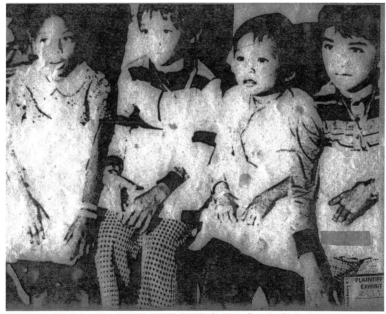

OPERATION BABYLIFT KIDS IN CARGO SECTION OF THE C5-A GALAXY

CHAPTER FOUR

The Vietnam War was a sour topic for most of us in high school. Just about every week someone in school knew or was related to a soldier who was killed in Vietnam. A lot of us feared graduation knowing that Vietnam awaited us. The first soldier I knew who died in Vietnam was Arthur Weary's first cousin, Johnny Blackmon. Johnny was a Marine who was drafted in 1966 and eventually went to Vietnam. His company came under hostile enemy fire in Quang Nam Province, South Vietnam on May 5, 1967. Johnny was hit by small arms fire and eventually died from his wounds at only 26 years old. He attained the rank of Corporal. His loss was a total shock to all of us; we had looked at Johnny as the invincible man.

I remember Johnny coming home to Flint once, dressed in his polished dress blue uniform, standing tall, black, and handsome. Every kid in our neighborhood admired him and some wanted to be a Marine when they grew up. In those days many of us thought that the Marines had the best looking uniforms out of all the services.

One such kid who was influenced by Johnny was James Carr. James, a year older than I, lived across the street from us. After graduation from high school James was drafted and became a Marine. James was a short fella and very quiet growing up. I was surprised to learn that he had become a Marine. James came home on leave one day in his dress blues. He looked like a totally different person, fit, sharp, well spoken, and walking with authority and pride. It was the summer of 1970. I had just graduated from high school in June of the same year.

James was home on leave right before he was deployed to Vietnam, on August 26, 1970. On September 17, 1970, James's platoon came under hostile fire in Quang Nam Province, South Vietnam. While parachuting into the war zone he sustained multiple fragmentation wounds and died on the battlefield. He was in Vietnam less than one month before he died fighting for our country.

James was only 19 years old and his rank was a private with the United States Marine Corps. His loss really hit home for me. His brother Lawrence and I were close friends and their family took his death very hard.

About six months later another friend from our neighborhood, Roy Dukes, was drafted. The United States Army drafted Roy sometime in November 1970 and he began his tour of duty in Vietnam on January 2, 1971. On March 3, 1971, Roy was based at Phuoc Long Province, South Vietnam, where his squadron came under ground attack. Roy died that same day, at age 20, but not from enemy engagement.

I enlisted in the United States Air Force the year after Roy was drafted. I didn't know that Roy died in Vietnam until I came home on leave for the first time in February 1971. I was saddened about the news of Roy dying and knew that someday I would go to Vietnam as well. My career field kept me out of harm's way, but any time that one is in the war theater anything can happen.

I was a junior in high school when Donald Clark, a neighborhood friend came home on leave from the U.S. Air Force. I sought his advice about life in the Air Force. He had been in the Air Force a few years and home on leave a few times. His advice weighed heavily on my decision to join the Air Force. It was rare to see a black man in an Air Force uniform in my neighborhood.

Donald was a very intelligent young man and someone whom I always admired growing up. I asked him if it was hard to join the Air Force, and he said no, all you need to do is pass the Air Force examination. He went on to say that he thought that I was Air Force material and I would do well once I got in.

When I turned 18 I received a high draft classification and I knew I would be drafted right out of high school. My plan was to try and get a job with GM after high school so if I got drafted, I would have a job when I got out of the service. Unfortunately, I was unable to get hired at GM. I went to the Air Force recruiter and applied to take the AF test, which I took two weeks later and passed. That was one of the most exciting days of my young life. I felt a sense of accomplishment by passing the AF test.

I left Flint and moved to Detroit later that summer and lived with my Aunt Doll. She tried to get me a job at Chrysler, but once again I couldn't get hired. By this time my draft classification number was close to being called. So, I went to the recruiter's office in Detroit and enlisted in the U.S. Air Force. This was in September of 1970 and my enlistment date was November 2, 1970. Donald Clark had given me very good advice when it came to the Air Force. In making that decision, I set myself up for the best and worst times of my life.

**RECIEVING AIRMAN'S MEDAL FROM
GENERAL PAUL K. CARLTON
(COMMANDER OF MILITARY AIRLIFT COMMAND)**

JOURNAL ENTRY
FEBRUARY 1975

- *I ask for a wake up call at 0400 hours, and boy does it come early. The CQ knocks on my door precisely at 0400 hours. I pop out of bed, take my shower, and put on my uniform. My uniform shirt is freshly starched, my pants are neatly creased and my shoes have a fresh spit shine. I call a taxi and ride to my squadron. Once there, I check the scheduling office to find out who I am flying with. Lt. Marcie Wirtz, Lt. Harriet Goffinet, SSgt. Gene Siddoway, TSgt. Dave Harris and I are the flight crew for flight 1621. We receive our briefing from the pilot and the MCD (Medical Crew Director) and go through our pre-flight check list and inspect the airplane. Our briefing includes going over each patient's charts and making sure the right equipment will accompany the flight. There is no special equipment needed for this mission.*

- *There are positions for two nurses and three med techs. Marcie is at the MCD post and Harriet is at 2nd nurse. I am SMT (senior med tech); Siddoway flies the 2nd med-tech position and Dave flies the third med-tech position. Each position has its own set of responsibilities.*

- The MCD is in charge of the medicine, the second nurse's duties include patient care and administering medications. The SMT duties include cooking meals, assisting the MCD, and directing the second and third med tech on additional responsibilities. The third med tech is in charge of baggage handling and patient care during flight. After completion of the preflight check list we board our aircraft and the pilot and his flight team go over our flight itinerary. We depart Clark AB at 0600 hours and in route to Yokota AB Japan with a four -hour flight time.

- This is a great flight team and I enjoy working with each one of them. Dave Harris is giving me a "check ride" on this Japan trip and I have no idea it is coming. Passing a "check ride" is essential because if you fail, you are grounded and risk retraining and loss of flying time and you only get flight pay when you fly missions. A "check ride" is when a flight examiner rates the aero medical evacuation technician on his skills with the use of equipment and in-flight performance with patient care. He gives a "check ride" to any the med tech unannounced.

- On our next flight to Japan Chief Master Sergeant Leon Jones decides to give an unannounced check ride to SSgt.

TK Jones. I am flying the third med tech position and TK is flying the SMT position. Chief Jones is our NCOIC (non commissioned officer in charge) of our squadron. On that flight we have the "big dog" examining one of our crew members. Chief Jones has been in aerovac for many years and he truly earned his wings. In other words he knows his stuff.

- *I am pretty nervous knowing that Chief Jones is flying out with us on our Japan mission. I have never flown with him before and I am just getting adjusted to being on flying status freshly out of flight school. Chief Jones is a very cool guy and he gets along with everybody in our squadron. We leave Clark AB headed for Yokota AB Japan to begin our pick-up of patients and passengers with in route stops before heading back to Clark.*

- *While observing TK performing his in-flight duties, Chief Jones is taking notes. You never know whether or not you passed your check ride until you get back to Clark. Normally, on Japan runs the crew will RON (remain over night) before flying back to Clark with in route stops along the way.*

- *We arrive back at Yokota after a long day of flying. Chief Jones asks if I want to have dinner and hang out at a local club in Shinjuku, a little town near Tokyo. Naturally, I say yes! We check into billeting quarters and get our rooms and get cleaned up and then hit the road. It's now after duty hours and we drop the protocol with addressing each other by rank and now it's on a first name basis.*

- *Leon (Chief Jones) says he has a friend in Shinjuku that owns a club and they serve terrific soul food. We all agree to go there, have a few beers and eat some soul food. Like I said before Leon is cool, and so is his partner. This guy is retired from the US Air Force and has set up a successful business in Japan. His club has more Japanese customers than American customers. The club has lockers available to store personal items; he serenades the customers with smooth jazz music. I am totally amazed at the history that he and Leon have. We have so much fun that night out with our boss, I will never be nervous around him again. TK passes his check ride with flying colors .*

- *Japan trips are always fun and basically each trip becomes a shopping trip. Most of the crew go stereo shopping at a local stereo store near the base named Phony's. Phony's carries the latest in stereo equipment, Sony Trinitron*

TV's, cameras, designer watches and a host of other goodies. I make sure to bring my girl something back on each trip to Japan. Life in Aero Medical Evacuation is the best.

CHAPTER FIVE

The Vietnam War ended in 1973. The Paris peace agreement was signed Jan. 27, 1973 by all parties to end the war. Henry Kissinger laid the ground work in Paris for the pull-out Oct. 26, 1972. The US started pulling out of Vietnam in the same year. America's withdrawal from South Vietnam began and the North Vietnamese started launching offensives soon after. The Paris peace agreement was violated immediately after we pulled out. The South Vietnamese government was unable to stop the advances from the North. Many South Vietnamese soldiers shredded their uniforms and melted into the population during the communist North Vietnamese onslaught toward the south.

South Vietnamese battalions were joining refugees fleeing the communist offensive. The US feared that South Vietnamese soldiers would not hold the North Vietnamese forces once we left. We pulled out most of our combat forces and mainly provided air support for the South Vietnamese soldiers. North Vietnamese forces were taking town after town starting with Ban Me Thoute and taking over coastal towns such as Cam Ram Bay.

The North Vietnamese forces had their eyes set on capturing the big prize, the capital city of Saigon. Communist forces were advancing from village to village and people were pouring into the highways trying to go south to Saigon. Kids were left homeless along the way and many died. Some had been abandoned and others were orphaned when their parents were killed by the communist forces. Hundreds of orphans in the northern part of South Vietnam started fleeing toward Saigon trying to escape the pursuing forces.

Mothers of Amer-Asian kids frequently took the children to orphanages hoping that they would be saved or adopted. The problem was many of the orphanages were over-filled with abandoned children. The further away from Saigon they were the harder it was to travel south on the congested highways. Communist forces had cut off some of the thoroughfares to prevent people from escaping, creating a serious humanitarian disaster with people fighting each other trying to hop on buses and trucks. The best form of transportation was motor bikes that could maneuver through traffic and avoid land mines that were on many roads.

Most of the US forces had pulled out by the end of 1974, leaving only military advisers behind. The communist forces were rapidly taking over military regions. The South Vietnamese forces essentially gave up the fight.

Da Nang overflowed with refugees very quickly and its airport teemed with people trying to flee to Saigon where they hoped to eventually leave the country. Countless orphans, many dazed and abandoned, were stuck at the airport in Da Nang. The US Embassy was flooded with calls asking for help in evacuating them. Initially, Graham Martin, the US Ambassador to South Vietnam, could not get authorization from Washington DC to evacuate the orphans.

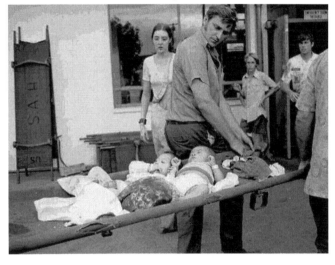

CHRISTIE LIEVERMANN AND SSGT. JAMES HADLEY RESCUE BABYLIFT KIDS FROM CRASH SITE, TAKEN TO SEVENTH DAY ADVENTIST HOSPITAL IN SAIGON

(Photo courtesy of Larry Engelmann & Tony Coalson)

CHAPTER SIX

Ed Daly, a Defense contractor, was the CEO of World Airways; he flew cargo in and out of Da Nang and witnessed the influx of orphans coming into Da Nang from the north. Daly volunteered to use his aircraft to fly some of the orphans to Saigon. There were so many orphans, Daly was overwhelmed and asked the US government for help.

When the US government was slow to react to this crisis, Daly started his unofficial Operation Babylift. He flew the first group of orphans to Oakland California without the approval of the US and Vietnamese governments. But Daly ran into serious trouble with President Ford when he landed in Oakland. Daly was making plans to go back to Vietnam to get more orphans, but President Ford decided that the government should be in charge of such a mission, and he announced the official Operation Babylift on April 3, with the first flight set for April 4, 1975.

President Ford announced Operation Babylift as a humanitarian mission that was set up to rescue Amer-Asian orphans out of Saigon. The evacuation continued well after the C-5A Galaxy crash. Operation Babylift successfully airlifted more than 2,500 orphans out of Vietnam. The crash of the C-5A Galaxy was the only exception. The civilian airlines – Pan Am, Flying Tigers, United Airlines and others, stepped in and volunteered to help complete the mission. The C-5A Galaxy was grounded pending an investigation into the cause of the crash, so a USAF C-141 cargo plane continued the Air Force Flights

Saigon fell soon after the last Operation Babylift flight, and refugees fled Vietnam not knowing where to go. Many got on flights to Clark Air Base, which became a central holding point for refugees and orphans passing through trying to get to the west to re-settle. Tents were set up on base as temporary housing, and many Babylift kids were cared for at the base gymnasium with military wives and dependents attending to them. Lois Boutwell, wife of Olen Boutwell, spent many hours as a volunteer. Olen survived in the troop compartment of the C-5A Galaxy crash and flew another mission the very next day while his wife cared for orphans at Clark.

Some children had families and others were alone but looking to reunite with their loved ones. The Philippines government approved the temporary entry into their country only for re-settlement, and the majority of the refugees camped out at Clark Air Base. I was told that most of the Vietnamese did not have any personal belongings. Only the affluent refugees had gold, jewelry and US dollars with them. They were able to use their valuables to barter their exodus to the west. The Vietnamese currency was worthless; much of the Vietnamese dong was thrown away.

Adoption agencies had parents from all over the world wanting to adopt the Babylift kids. The majority of the orphans were sent from Clark Air Base to Denver Colorado where adults were waiting to bring them to their new homes. At the same time, we read and heard stories of kids being stolen by people who tried to bypass the legal channels.

But no one rushed to adopt the handicapped, physically and mentally challenged children or the malnourished ones.

Remarkably, most of the orphans were adopted into loving families all over the world. It's a great feeling to know that I played a small part in bringing some of them to safety. I think about my fallen crew members who sacrificed their lives for the freedom of so many kids. I needed to share my story no matter how painful it was.

It took me a lot of years to get through the emotional trauma of surviving an airplane crash -- a five minute window that changed my life forever.

Poem:
 At 0655...I was alerted to fly in Vietnam's not so friendly skies...
 Where too many died... But not Phil Wise...
I had often wondered why... It was just meant for me to survive...
In God's glory I'm able to tell my story! Thank you Lord!

**WORLD AIRWAYS OPERATION BABYLIFT RESCUE
(APRIL 1975)
(Courtesy of Larry Englemann)**

JOURNAL ENTRY
FEBRUARY 1975

- *SSgt. Harris quietly sits at the third med tech seat and tells me that he will grade me on how well I perform the SMT position throughout this mission. The flight to Japan is smooth and we fly dead head, which means that no patients and just a few passengers are on board. Leaving out of Clark is typically easy and it's a time for some of us to get some sleep. Sleepy as I am, I cannot sleep because I am being monitored throughout the entire flight by SSgt. Harris. The SMT seat is in the aft of the aircraft and it faces the passenger seats, so if you doze off or nod off to sleep everyone can see you. It is so hard staying awake especially when the seatbelt light is illuminated and when we are in turbulent weather. I have to remain seated, so drinking more coffee is out of the question.*

- *Finally we arrive at our first of four stops, Misawa AB Japan; flight time is about four hours. And as SMT I'm responsible for announcing our arrival over the PA system, which I do. We have to pick up 10 people at the first stop: four litter patients, six ambulatory patients and two passengers. Our ground time is less than 20 minutes and we* are off to our next stop, Yokosuka NAS, where we on load three litter patients, five ambulatory patients, and six passengers. So far on this trip, we have taken no seriously injured patients on board. Our next stop is Yokota AB; flight time about one hour thirty minutes. Yokota is the last stop before heading back to the Philippines tomorrow. The crews have to get mandatory crew rest so we remain over night at Yokota AB.

- After shutting down the aircraft and checking into the billeting quarters, I shower and head to Phony's, the very popular stereo center. My best friend Maurice Ellison is stationed at Tachikawa AB, which neighbors Yokota AB; he picks me up from billeting quarters and takes me to some unknown Japanese back alley restaurant where the food is just fantastic.

- Whenever I ask Maurice how he finds such places to eat; he simply says, "I follow my nose." After dinner we head back to Maurice's place. Maurice and his wife Mary are newlyweds and have been in Japan less than a year. I haven't seen them in a few weeks since my last trip but it is always a blast. After a few shots of sake (rice wine) and a couple of chess games, I have him drop me off back at the base billeting.

- *It's Wednesday morning and crew rest is over and now we have breakfast and board the aircraft to prepare it for enplaning of patients and passengers for our final leg to Clark AB. Before we leave from Japan, I check with the third med tech to make sure the stereo equipment that we purchased from Phony's is on board. This is important because the value and the name brand of the equipment had to be claimed for customs upon arrival to Clark AB Republic of the Philippines.*

- *Once back at Clark all of our patients are off loaded on to a bus and taken to the base hospital where they stay overnight awaiting transportation back to the States. My Japan trip has come to an end and the rest of the day I am on crew rest.*

CHAPTER SEVEN

When I graduated from Southwestern High School in Flint in 1970, I knew I had two choices: Go to college or go to Vietnam. The Vietnam War was raging, not only in the rice paddies of Vietnam, but on American soil, as well. An outspoken public showed their distinct displeasure with America's involvement in a war thousands of miles away.

America's youth made their feelings known with protests and marches. One such protest at Kent State University in Ohio led to the death of a student who was shot by a National Guardsman. That incident only fueled the fire of disdain toward the war, which I was sure that I was going to enter. Although I considered myself a pretty smart kid, my high school grades weren't quite what they should be in order to get into college. So, I knew that eventually I would be drafted. I decided to enlist in the United States Air Force. Looking back, that was undoubtedly the smartest move I had ever made in my then young life.

By enlisting in the Air Force, I was able to gain at least a little control over my future in regards to where I would be serving. And that was a good thing because at the time I wanted no part of Vietnam. In those days, the Army drafted you and the Marines chose you. The Navy and Air Force were all volunteer branches of service, if you could pass the test to get in. Fortunately, I was able to pass the Air Force tests.

Bernice Chatman Davis, my Aunt Doll, played a major role in my decision to join the Air Force. I lived with her at the time I was thinking about enlisting. I couldn't find work in Detroit and I was becoming more and more restless. My aunt and I had a conversation about my future.

"What do you want to do?" she asked.

I told her I had a high draft classification and it was very likely that I would be drafted, and that I had passed the Air Force examination in Flint. Also, time was running out for me to decide and that I was leaning toward enlistment in the Air Force.

"Well, honey, looks like you've made your decision and I support you." It was that conversation with her that sealed the deal for me. I thank her for supporting me and I love her very much.

After I decided to sign up I had to go to Historic Fort Wayne, in Detroit, to take a physical exam, the oath, and sign my enlistment papers. Although it eventually turned out to be one of the greatest experiences of my life, I had lots of mixed emotions during the bus ride to Historic Fort Wayne. I was elated at having passed the rigorous battery of tests, and I was also thinking that maybe I had just signed my life away. It was hard to keep negativity out of my mind as I listened to some of the other people on the bus, crying and regretting their decision.

Finally, after we were processed and cleared the induction center at Historic Fort Wayne, reality hit. "We are your momma and daddy now," one of the officers said. From there, we boarded a bus to the Detroit Metropolitan Airport to catch a flight headed for Lackland AFB.

I was 18-years old and a newly enlisted airman heading to basic training at Lackland AFB, San Antonio, Texas. I remember getting off the bus as it pulled up to the administration center. Our training instructor, Technical Sergeant Tippler, met our bus and ordered the men on our flight to fall in line and he took role call. I was nervous and a bit frightened because TSgt. Tippler was a tough, demanding, airman. He immediately got everyone's attention with an intimidating voice. He would get in our faces and shout and dare us to say anything. He established who the boss was right away.

Basic training lasted six weeks. I had a little trouble adjusting to military training and class courses pertaining to military rules and regulations. Everything was so strict and everything had to be perfect. There was no room for failure and excuses. The first two weeks of basic training were the most difficult. We were introduced to a grueling regime, and I was not ready for it at all. Not only was I out physically out of shape but I was homesick. I questioned my decision more than once in those first weeks.

To prepare myself for each grueling day, I would take a cold shower every morning. My fellow trainees thought I was a little crazy. But, that proved to be a very effective way for me to stay sharp, alert and awake during early classes where I tended to get sleepy. During our rare down time I managed to keep myself busy by shining shoes for other trainees, for a small fee, of course.

For a time during basic training, I thought I might not make it because I had difficulty learning how to square corners when marching. Thank God, I figured it out. Learning how to salute took me a while, too. TSgt. Tippler took me aside to work with me. Needless to say I learned how to salute very well. Before I nailed it, I would go out of my way to avoid officers so I would not have to salute them. Once I learned, I purposefully put myself in their paths so I could salute.

In basic training I didn't have a girlfriend like other trainees who received letters almost daily. My mother and I corresponded as my training progressed. Mail call was pretty lonely for me most of the time. I once received a letter from Denise, a girl I liked in Detroit. Denise lived across the street from my Aunt Doll. Needless to say, that made my day. Nothing serious came of our friendship, but it was nice to hear from her. I called her a couple of times, and it helped me get through those lonely days. It's amazing how a simple act of kindness can make such a big difference in a person's life. I had no clue how life was going to really teach me that lesson.

I was thrilled to have graduated from the technical school at Sheppard Air Force Base in Texas and to be assigned to Wilford Hall Medical Center, Lackland Air Force Base, the Air Force's largest medical facility.

The first time I saw someone die, I was working in the Intensive Care Unit. Our patient was an 18-year-old airman in basic training who caught pneumonia. He was from Idaho, training in the hot Texas sun in February, and came down with a severe cold. We worked with him for several weeks, but his condition never improved once pneumonia set in. I was saddened by his death. Only a few short months before, it could have been me getting sick coming from a cold state like Michigan and going through basic training in November in San Antonio. I felt sorry that he died so young while still in training.

Soon after that young airman died another pneumonia patient came into ICU. This patient was much older and ready to retire from the US Air Force. I won't mention his name, but my buddy (Maurice Ellison) and I named him Herman. Herman was a fighter; he would not give up even when the doctors lost hope.

Herman went into cardiac arrest so many times, it got to the point where it seemed as though he could go into cardiac arrest on command. Herman became our friend after many weeks in ICU, and Maurice and figured out how to help him. He wasn't able to talk because he had a tracheotomy, but each time he was experiencing discomfort Maurice would try to sooth him. If that failed, Maurice would tell the nurse to administer morphine, and our man Herman would smile. We noticed each time we mentioned morphine, Herman would smile. We would say to him we know you like taking morphine, we know you like seeing pink elephants when you are high. And Herman would smile.

Several times, doctors wanted to pull the plug because Herman had been defibrillated so many times and wasn't getting better. He actually had pad marks all over his chest from where he'd been defibrillated. One morning during our nurses' briefing, Maurice and I shared with the staff our observation about our friend Herman.

We explained that we thought Herman was hooked on morphine and that he was too high to do his daily physical therapy. The nurses began decreasing his morphine and he was awake more and more. As we got him out of bed more frequently, Herman got stronger and stronger and made a full recovery. When Herman came back to Wilford Hall ICU to visit us, he thanked us and told us he had heard everything we were saying. "I saw many pink elephants," he said with a smile. And Maurice and I could hardly stop laughing.

My first job assignment was as a medical technician on a cardiology ward. I worked ICU and CCU (Coronary Care Unit) and rotated between the ward and the special care units. Eventually I went on to work with patients at one of the many modulars that housed drug patients from Southeast Asia. These patients had to go through drug detoxification from their heroin addiction. Many of them had serious problems outside of drug addictions – other health issues, dishonorable discharge, and even criminal charges. Our goal was to get them off drugs and reacquaint them to civilian life.

CLARK AIR BASE REPUBLIC OF THE PHILIPPINES

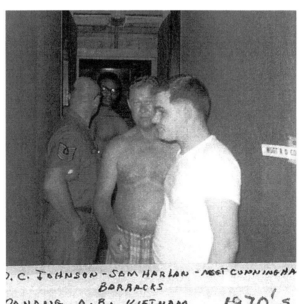

DENNING C. JOHNSON
(PHOTO COURTESY OF ROBERT ST. MAUR)

CHAPTER EIGHT

The first day at my barracks was December 1971. I was carrying my luggage walking toward my room when I heard the sounds of a saxophone in the hallway. The closer I got to my room I heard a guitar mixing it up, too. I stood in the hallway listening to the music coming from a room with the door slightly ajar. The musicians stopped jamming when they saw me standing outside, and they invited me in. I introduced myself and met Maurice Ellison, Mary Rodriquez, and Maurice's roommate John Rocher. Maurice and Mary were dating. Mary is a beautiful Spanish woman with roots in Chicago. In those days we had so much fun together. Maurice played the saxophone and Rocher played guitar. We were all jazz enthusiasts. Eventually, Maurice and Mary got married and started a family. Maurice and I became best friends, and he and Mary named me godfather to their first daughter, Erica.

I had a sense of freedom and liberation when I got my first apartment. I maintained my room on base in the dormitory as well, which was convenient for when I had to work. But at the apartment I could really relax and enjoy myself. I must say, my friends and I had a lot of parties there.

From time to time, I would hustle pool (pocket billiards) with Bruce, who was a good buddy of mine. Bruce was a white guy with very good pool skills, and my pool game was equal to his. We would get together and go to the Airman's club to hustle pool. We lived in the same barracks and that's where we would plot our strategy. Bruce would play against the brothers for money, and Bruce would win all the time. I would stay out of the game when Bruce was hustling these guys. The game was nine ball with multiple players. When Bruce got ahead in winnings, I would enter the game. This is when I would get on a winning roll. The brothers would cheer for me thinking that I was winning their money back. In other words they didn't mind losing to me.

Keep in mind they didn't know Bruce and I were hustling them. We would come out of the game as winners and would go back to the barracks and split our winning. This hustle went on for a while without detection. I was able to keep extra money in my pockets and often I didn't have to use cash from my paycheck. I continued playing pool or pocket billiards all during my Air Force career.

I didn't limit my hustling pool to the base; I played pool quite often on the east side of San Antonio. I would always take someone with me to watch my back, mainly Maurice or my roommate Theodore Lee. It was hard getting pool action when your game was strong. So, if you showed your game before playing for money chances are no one would bet with you.

What I would do is go into the pool hall and make a game shooting with my left hand. I'm right handed. That way, if anyone is checking me out, my real game is disguised. This formula often worked against first-time opponents. Obviously, I was not that good shooting pool with my left hand. My opponents figured they could beat me after watching me play, losing occasionally.

Usually a player approached me to make a game, thinking he had an easy hustle. I had a habit of telling my opponent that I was good, just to protect myself because I knew how things would end up. We would start off betting low wagers; remember, I'm shooting with my left hand. I would fall behind and not compete up to par. My opponent would get cocky and increase the bet. Naturally, I would agree but I would request an extra premium in wagers in order to get my money back.

When the money got right, I would switch hands. The stakes were high enough for me to re-coup what I'd lost in one game. I would be on a winning roll before the opponent realized what was happening but it would be too late for him. Next, I had to think about making my exit, and that's when things always got a little complicated. At this point I would be so happy I brought my buddies with me. My opponents would yell out, "You hustler" over and over again, and I would signal to my friends to leave, right away.

Going back to the base was fun; I had made a little money, and executed my plans perfectly. I had a lot of good days in San Antonio, and hustling pool became very lucrative. I became confident knowing I could make extra money playing pool. It came in handy when military pay day was every two weeks.

The fondest memory from those days was buying my first car, a used 1966 burgundy Chevy Corvair with black-wall tires. Having a car allowed me a type of freedom I'd never known before. I saved my money and paid $600 in cash for it. Having a car meant so much to me, I felt liberated and I could go and come at will and not depend on others for transportation. I loved that car! It had the engine in the back and trunk in the front of the car. I bought it from Bill, a co-worker who was transferring to another base and needed to sell it. Needless to say, the car paid for itself in no time because I was able get around and hustle pool any time I felt like it.

The Airman's club was a treasure trove of suckers that liked to bet on pool. I would just hang out there quietly and get paid. I felt so blessed having a permanent assignment in San Antonio and the freedom of being an adult with a job and resources. The Air Force made a man out of me and I was proud to wear my uniform and serve my country.

**GENERAL PAUL K. CARLTON PINNING ON THE
AIRMAN'S MEDAL**

JOURNAL ENTRY
JANUARY 1975

- *It's the second week of January and I'm scheduled for a trip to Thailand. I begin the week by performing alert duties Monday and flying out Wednesday on a run to Thailand. This trip is one of my favorites because Thailand is known in the aerovac circle as a country where beautiful women are plentiful and bar hopping is the thing to do. It's also known for it jewelry, leather goods and local cuisine. Our stay is normally short and we only remain over night (RON).*

- *Wednesday's here. I stayed at my apartment the night before. I've been up practically all night partying and bar hopping. When it comes time to fly I am hung over or tired from drinking too many San Miguel beers. I struggle to clear my head up for the 0400 hours wake up time, but once I take a long hot shower I am okay.*

- *Showtime is at 0500 hours and I have just enough time to run to the chow hall for breakfast, which is right near the barracks. I catch a taxi to the squadron after breakfast and attend our morning briefing. Our flight assignment is a mission to Thailand. We are to pick up patients at four different stops. We arrive at Udorn Air Base, our first stop.*

We take on six litter patients, 12 ambulatory patients, and no passengers. Within 20 minutes we are airborne again in route to Ubon Air Base, Thailand, about a 55 minute flight. We go onto Takli and Utapao Air Base to pick up more patients and passengers before returning to Clark Air Base, Philippines.

- Flying into Thailand is often a grueling trip; we really, really work hard. We frequently fly back with an airplane full of patients and passengers. I am humiliated upon returning to Clark Air Base. A customs official always boards the aircraft for inspection, most of the time walking through and collecting the custom declaration forms.

- On this trip the K-9 dogs meet the aircraft. It is not unusual for the K-9 dogs to inspect aircrafts coming from Thailand, because a lot of drugs are coming from Thailand and the Asian triangle. On this particular trip back home, the Air Force Security Police and Customs representative direct all of the crew to retrieve their own luggage, and form a line, then stand next to our bags. We are standing on the flight line near the aircraft when suddenly I see this huge black and tan German Sheppard Police dog with his handler. The dog is beautiful, but fierce looking as he sits there. The handler and his K-9 begin their *search of our luggage, with the dog walking by each crew member and his bags, including mine.*

- *The dog handler comes to search me for a third time and not the others; he brings the dog to me again. At this point, I speak up, jokingly. I say, "Why do you keep bringing your dog to me? Is it because I'm the only black guy on the crew?" At this point he stops his inspection and clears all of us to leave. I stand there thinking, what just happened? Why was I singled out? I'm wondering if the crew thought I was a smuggler or something. I don't know, all I can say is that I feel embarrassed, humiliated, and confused. (Strangely it never happens again on searches after any subsequent return flights from Thailand.)*

- *There are very few blacks in aerovac and I am fortunate to be a part of aeromedical evacuation; it is a great job. While I am based at Clark Air base, we are required to attend a race relation classes. Today in class, we are asked to identify stereotyping or racially insensitive commercials on TV. The class has a majority of whites and a few blacks. Not any of the whites note one such commercial or give any examples.*

- *One black airman raises his hand, and asks, "Why don't they have black hair commercials?" Another black guy asks,*

"Why are blacks portrayed as cooks on products such as Uncle Ben's Minute Rice or Aunt Jemima Pancakes or Mrs. Butterworth Syrup but are not used to advertise other products?" These are provocative questions to most of the whites. I have my own question and raise my hand. I ask, "Why is it that on those band-aid commercials the band-aids always match white folks and not black folks' skin?" Right away everyone smiles as though a light switch has come on. I feel like some of them really get it or understand where I am coming from.

CHAPTER NINE

Without question, the greatest thing that happened to me during my career in the Air Force was meeting Tessie, the woman who would become my wife and mother of our beautiful daughter, La Nika. Tessie's given name is Sufriana, but I've always called her Tessie. I remember how we first met as if it was yesterday.

I had just completed flight school in March 1973 with orders to Clark Air Force Base, in the Republic of the Philippines. This was part of my plan and set the ground work for me meeting Tessie, and I have to thank my buddy Mac Daniel for that. Mac was my supervisor when I worked at the Drug Rehabilitation Center at Lackland Air Force Base.

Soldiers had to go to rehab to detoxify from the heroin addiction that was rampant in Vietnam, Thailand and the entire Asian triangle. Mac would always talk to me about his girlfriend, Lee, who lived in the Philippines. Mac had shown me many pictures of her, and she was a beautiful Filipina woman with long black hair who adored Mac. After seeing photos of Lee, and talking to his girl over the phone, I fantasized about meeting a Filipina woman, too. I was only 20 years old and had no steady girlfriend, so I was looking for a relationship.

One day Mac asked me if I wanted to go to the Philippines. He said he could make it happen. Of course, I said yes, and going there would be a dream come true. Mac had a good friend who worked at Randolph Air Force Base in Texas. Randolph handled Air Force personnel assignments. It was December of 1972, and to my surprise I received orders for a new assignment. The orders read: Report to Brooks School of Aero Space Medicine, San Antonio, Texas, and after completion report to the Ninth Aero Medical Evacuation Group Clark Air Force Base, Republic of the Philippines.

That was great news for me. I had official orders to the Philippines and couldn't wait to share the news with Mac. I saw him later and I shouted, "I got my orders to the P.I.! Thank you! Mac! Thank you!" He just smiled and winked at me.

Then he reminded me that I had to make it through flight school in order to get there. Let me tell you, there was no way I wasn't going to pass flight school. Because I knew when I put my mind to it I could do anything. I passed flight school training with no problem during six weeks of intensive training. I learned everything one could possibly want to know about treating a patient in the air including how the body reacts to certain altitudes.

Then it was on to the Philippines and Clark AFB. I arrived at Clark on April 7, 1973. It was high noon when we touched down and the doors opened for deplaning. The blistering heat shimmered in waves along the flight line. I went through two days of orientation learning about the customs and laws of the host country. We learned where to avoid going, and about different hustlers who preyed on Americans new to the country once they were outside the base.

On the third day in the PI (Philippine Islands) I met William, a fellow airman who had been stationed at Clark for a year. William offered to take me off base with him to meet his girlfriend, Cora. I had never been off base before and was a little reluctant about going. The stories I'd heard left me thinking twice being off base. William convinced me he had my back. He also said that Cora had a friend, and asked if I would be interested in meeting her. I agreed, and we made our way to the main gate and caught a jeepney, which was an old World War II jeep that was modified into a passenger vehicle. The jeepney could hold up to 10 people.

We rode the jeepney to Diamond Subdivision. Diamond Subdivision had a strip with bars, hotels, places to shop, and restaurants. William and I began walking down the street and saw William's girlfriend and another girl with her. They were riding on their bikes and Cora was smiling enthusiastically, as she glanced over at her girlfriend who was glaring at us. William introduced his girlfriend and her friend, my future wife, to me: "Phil, this is Cora and she has her friend with her that I want you to meet," he said. "Her name is Tessie."

I was stunned by the sheer beauty of Tessie. She had long, black, shiny hair that fell well below her knees. She was well kept, with a gorgeous manicure and pedicure. She was as pretty as any Hollywood starlet, but as I would soon discover, she had a beautiful heart as well. Tessie was no doubt the total package.

Tessie explained to me that she had a boyfriend. But the fact she had a boyfriend meant absolutely nothing to me, because from the moment I met her, I knew she was the woman for me. The four of us agreed to meet later that day for dinner, and as we were leaving William asked Cora for a good-bye kiss. Cora puckered up and laid a big kiss on him. Of course, I felt I needed a goodbye kiss, too. So I looked at Tessie and smiled, expecting a goodbye kiss. But Tessie was guarded. After all, she had just met me, and I am sure she was still thinking about her boyfriend.

But I must admit I was a rather charming guy back then, and fortunately my charms won her over. Although she was a bit reluctant, she fell for my charms and turned her face and motioned for me to kiss her cheek. But that was not good enough for me. I stole a kiss on her lips. I kissed her gently, and I knew then that I was in love. From that point on our relationship grew, and she fell in love with me. And even after 34 years of marriage, I can't believe how blessed I am that this beautiful woman fell in love with me. A lesson one can take from this experience is "Persistence beats resistance. See something you want and never give up; go for it."

Tessie's from an island in the southern Philippines called Negros Orientals. She left home as a young lady to come to Manila, where she lived with her cousin Dael. In Manila she was able to earn money for herself and her family back home in Negros. Her life in Manila was tough, and she was involved in a bad relationship, but that relationship produced two adoring boys, Ronald and Roderick that she loved dearly. After getting out of that abusive relationship,

Tessie made a decision to take her sons and move to Angeles City, located near Clark Air Force Base. I am forever grateful that she did.

Our relationship became more serious after she decided to leave her boyfriend. I was living on base at the time and it wasn't long before I found an apartment off base. We eventually moved in together and her boys stayed in Negros Orientals where they attended school and lived with her mother and sister. In July 1973, I went to Negros Oriental province to visit her home in Opao (Tugas), a small barrio right off the main highway leading into the town of Tanjay City. I will never forget my first visit there.

Her family treated me with so much love. Of course they knew all about me long before they met me. Tessie and I flew in from Manila and were greeted by a host of family members. They just wanted to talk and practice their English in getting to know me. A couple of her family members wanted to touch my hair because they had not seen a black person before.

RONALD, RODERICK, LA NIKA,TESSIE AND PHIL

CHAPTER TEN

Another person who had a positive impact on my life is Howard Olson, part-owner of Michigan Lumber Company, located a few houses from where we lived on Clifford Street. My family had just moved from an apartment on Clifford Street into a house on the same street. And since I was the kind of kid always looking to make a buck, I went to the lumber company from time to time hoping I could find work. I started 'volunteering' to sweep the wood shavings and saw dust off the mill floor, and take on other odd tasks

Mr. Al, who did the cleaning around the lumberyard office building and who seemed to always be in a hurry, appreciated my help and would often give me a tip. I found out later that he was always in a hurry because he had a church that he ministered. Pretty soon I became a regular at the lumberyard. And for whatever reason Mr. Olson grew very fond of me. He started having me do all kinds of jobs around the place, his home and errands here and there. Mr. Olson knew he could call on me to do any of the jobs he needed done.

He would even let me drive his car around the lumberyard parking lot. In fact, that is where I learned to drive, and when I got old enough to get my license he would give me his car to run errands around town. My father was not letting me drive off in his car because we only had one and he needed it for work. Mr. Olson was always so supportive and encouraging. He helped build my self-confidence, and he wanted me to have a great future. He even told me that he would help pay for my college. What can you say about a person who exudes such generosity?

I really believe Mr. Olson grew so fond of me because of my honesty. Not long after I started hanging around the lumberyard, I was sweeping in the office area near the cash register. Sitting on the floor near the cash register was a $20 bill. It was just lying there waiting to be picked up. I could've easily slipped the money into my pocket, but I didn't. Instead, when I saw the money I immediately called Mr. Olson and let him know unaccounted for money was sitting out. When he came in and saw me holding that $20, he broke out into a smile. "Thank you, young man" he said. There was an extra sparkle on that kind man's face that day. And now that I look back on it, I really believe he was testing my honor and integrity. I think he was saying to himself, "Would this little boy steal from me?' The answer was "No." I never thought about putting that money in my pocket because it wasn't mine. From that day my relationship with Mr. Olson grew even stronger. And it would last up until the day he died.

Howard Olson kept up with me during my tour of duty with the United States Air Force. He was greatly affected when he read in our local paper about me being involved in an airplane crash in Vietnam. He wrote me a very touching letter that brought tears to my eyes as I read it lying in my hospital bed in the Philippines. I felt this man's love through the letter he wrote showing concern and wishing me a speedy recovery. In his letter, he told me that I would have a job with Michigan Lumber Company after completion of my service to my country. He didn't care about the type of injuries I sustained or the mental condition I was in, he just wanted to help me.

When I returned to Flint after I retired from the U.S. Air Force in 1977, I went to Michigan Lumber Company to check on Mr. Olson. He was tickled to see me; the smile on his face just glowed with pride and admiration. We hugged each other and we both began to shed tears. I was close with the entire office there at Michigan Lumber company. I reunited with Mr. Ralph who had played a role in shaping my character at the lumberyard; he trusted me and never doubted my ability. When I was younger Mr. Ralph would always give my brothers and me free nails or scrap wood to contribute to our tree house project. He was and is a genuinely good guy.

Mr. Olson was true to his word and hired me to work at the Lumber Company upon my return. As Mr. Olson grew older he retired from the Lumber Company and I moved on and went to college. Mr. Olson took sick and his family was unable to take care of him. When I learned that the family decided to place him in a nursing home, I became a regular visitor there. And I used all the nursing skills I had learned in the Air Force to make him as comfortable as possible when I was there, because he wasn't doing well physically. Not only that, I did not think the nursing home was taking good care of him; and I let them know that more than once when I would come by for a visit and smell a foul odor. Many times I took it upon myself to wash and shave Mr. Olson. It was the least I could do for the kindest man I know. Mr. Olson was my friend.

I learned a lot from my relationship with Howard Olson. He dispelled a lot of things I had heard about white people. Up until I met Mr. Olson, I was taught a white man never meant a black man any good. But this white man had taken an interest in a little black boy. He offered me kindness and generosity. Howard Olson was an excellent role model for me.

My wife worked for Howard Olson's uncle, Victor Olson. She was a caregiver for Victor Olsen and his wife Grace. Tessie cared for both Olsons until the end of their lives. Between watching my mother and father work hard and caring for us, and working for Mr. Vaughn and Howard Olson, I had strong, positive role models who taught me a work ethic and a sense of responsibility. Howard Olson passed on, but left me with a strong message about mankind: It doesn't matter what color you are; it's about integrity, trust, and empowerment of others. Those tenets still serve me well to this day.

MICHIGAN LUMBER COMPANY, CIRCA 1960s

Airlift crash injured Flintite

A U.S. Air Force sergeant from Flint who was aboard the C5 Galaxy transport plane that crashed in Vietnam while carrying war orphans bound for the U.S. is in fair condition with multiple fractures at Clark Air Force Base in the Philippines.

Philip R. Wise, a medical technician who was participating in President Ford's Operation Babylift, suffered multiple head and leg injuries and a bruised left eye, according to an Air Force telegram sent to his mother, Mrs. Minnie Vincent, 411 E. Twelfth St.

According to government reports, the crash of the C5 was caused when a rear cargo door blew out from "unknown causes."

The plane was carrying 243 orphans ranging in age from 8 months to 12 years; 44 U.S. Mission escorts; 16 Air Force crewmen; two flight nurses and 10 medics and nurses from the Philippines.

The plane took off from Saigon early Friday and was 40 to 60 miles from the capital en route to Clark Air Force Base when the cargo door blew out, according to reports.

The pilot attempted to turn back toward Tan Son Nhut Air Base but lost control, and the plane crashed in a swampy area just outside the base and exploded.

Of the 305 passengers, according to Saigon reports, at least 178 were killed, more than half of them children. It was the first crash of a C5.

The pilot of the plane was Air Force Maj. Dennis Traynor, whose parents, Mr. and Mrs. Dennis W. Traynor, live in Flushing. He also was among survivors.

Sgt. Philip R. Wise

1970, and his father, Roosevelt Wise Jr., 2926 Atherton Terrace said he heard from his son infrequently. His mother said she last saw her son when he came home last summer and found no jobs in Flint.

He enlisted in 1970 out of Southwestern High School and was promoted to sergeant during his first four-year tour. In 1972, he was stationed in the Philippines after basic training in Texas, his mother said, and frequently made flights to Japan, Thailand and other Asian countries.

When he couldn't find work after his first tour, his mother said, he re-enlisted and was again assigned to Clark Air

FLINT JOURNAL APRIL 5,1975

JOURNAL ENTRY
FEBRUARY 1975

- *During the next two weeks we fly routine missions including a flight to Vietnam. Flying into Vietnam is a priority because in order to receive one month's combat pay you have to fly "in country" at least once a month.*

- *February starts off with an urgent aerovac mission to Vietnam. I am on alert duty and it's about 0900 hours when I get the call; luckily I am on base. We are sent to pick up an urgent patient with head and chest wounds; he has to undergo surgery Stateside. Our leg is the first leg of this long journey to the USA. Our two-hour flight to Clark is busy, touch and go for a while with our patient. I read his chart and he sustained his injuries from a grenade blast earlier that day. He is only 19 years old and been in-country (Vietnam) only six weeks. When you see that, it's really heartbreaking and an honor to give your all when caring for our brave soldiers.*

- *We make it to Clark and off load our patient. There is a C-141 aircraft waiting to carry him and other patients home to the USA. The C-141 transport aircraft is designed for long flights such as crossing the Pacific Ocean. This is a familiar Aerovac route with the destination stop at Travis AFB California. I don't know if that soldier made it or not but I do know we did our jobs to get him to U.S. soil alive. That's the beauty of Aero Medical Evacuation: It shows our ability to airlift patients anywhere in the world.*

- *The rest of the month is a mix of routine missions to Korea, Japan, Okinawa, Thailand and Vietnam. On my last February mission (1975) I get the flight I want, a Japan run. My 23rd birthday is two weeks away. I need this run to shop for a few things for my girl Tessie. She loves for me to surprise her with gifts such as jade stones, jade jewelry, pearls and glass animals from Taiwan. Tessie is my jewel here on earth; wherever I go I shop for jewelry with her in mind. I buy my sake and Akadoma from Japan. I also buy a Korean wine named Oscar with a taste more like champagne, bubbly and good.*

CHAPTER ELEVEN

I used to love playing marbles. We played everywhere including the floor. We would play on the carpet too. We would take a piece of bar soap and make a circle on the carpet or floor. We used bar soap because it cleaned up good, and Mom would never know that we played marbles on her floors.

But we mostly played outside and I remember the day my great aunt, Aunt Sally, saved me from a horrible fate. I just knew I was gonna get a whipping because Momma could put up with a lot, but busting out the knees of some perfectly good pants playing marbles, well that was a whipping offense. I could barely lift my feet up the long steps going up to our apartment, knowing what was coming.

I should have been happy. I'd had a fantastic marble day. Only an hour or so had passed but it felt like days or weeks since I'd run out of the door holding prized marbles I'd pulled out of my "welfare spam meat" can -- a stinger and a few I could afford to lose. It had not taken long to find a game with Stevie and the other boys. We had four players and we each threw five marble in the circle. I stood up and shot mine into a circle full of marbles. I stuck my first shot and knelt down on my knees and began my run. I would shoot and break then get one out and go on a run.

I was cleaning up when I felt something up side my head. It was big old fat Vance or whatever he was calling himself today. He never would tell us his real name because he was always getting in trouble; but if anyone started his description with "big old, fat old," then everybody knew who was the culprit.

So there I am doubling my marbles that I brought out and he was trying to whack me in the head. He liked doing that, I thought. No, I knew. Something was wrong with him. So I tried to avoid him. And when I couldn't avoid him, I would confront him and lead him away from the sure violence that was coming. But he snuck up on me this morning and I didn't have anything. I was just there. Wide open with no defense. Just sure a butt-whipping of another kind was coming. And then SPLAT! A bird circled and let out a huge white load that hit Vance right in the top of his head. When it splattered, we fell out laughing. Vance wiped the bird poo off with his shirt sleeve and said, "I dare you, bird, I double dipping dare you to …" and just as he looked up the bird delivered an even bigger load right in his face.

We laughed so hard and it was a harsh reminder that Vance was just a kid too, only bigger and only lonelier and only scared of everybody bigger than him. So when he was the biggest, he struck first. But not that day. It was enough to break up the game and my winning streak, because the only other game I could find next was at the playground on the cement.

I preferred the dirt but every now and then I liked to stretch out and try different things; and I found out I was good at shooting on the cement, too. A whole bunch of boys were playing with a lot of marbles that could really roll in a very big circle, and I hit another lucky streak. A run like my daddy would do on the pool table in that social club under our apartment ... that very club whose window I peaked in as I dragged up the steps with holes in both my knees from scraping around on the cement.

But I'd done well. My pockets were bulging with marbles. I had even thought, as I was about to open the door, that I should have put some of them in my back pockets to pad the blow ... but I started smiling as I opened the door. It really was my lucky day. Aunt Sally was sitting on the sofa and she lit up like a light bulb when she saw me.

Aunt Sally lived in Hanford, California, (where I was born). I remember her visits to us in Michigan. She would always ask me to thread her needles. She had all the boys threading her needles (for quilt making), but I was pretty fast at threading the needle. The challenge of who can thread the needle the fastest was made into a game... She was getting ready to do some sewing and she was just getting ready to try and thread the needle. Her eye glasses were the biggest coke bottle-looking glasses I had ever seen, and she needed my help. I was only more than glad to help. I looked at my momma who looked at those two big holes in my pants, and then she looked at that big old smile on her aunt's face, and I knew I had escaped my anticipated fate. I could take my pants off and Aunt Sally would sew me new patches, and my momma wouldn't have to use that old iron off the stove and put on those iron-on patches that she hated.

The stove was a black cast iron one with a steel door. We used large black charcoal blocks inside it. When the coal truck delivered our coal, the boys had to unload and store it in the basement. I was glad that our next house had a stove that used heating oil.

Mom used those iron-on patches and her sewing kit a lot to repair our clothes when we were small. She taught me how to sew to repair my own clothes. Momma just looked at me with those torn knees and said, "Bet you thought you were going to get in trouble, didn't you?"

"Yes Ma'am" I replied.

"But you didn't," Aunt Sally chimed in. "Sometimes you just gotta have faith. Sometimes when it look like you got no which way to turn ... you just gotta have faith. Faith the size of a mustard seed can move mountains." I didn't understand what she said or why she said it but it stuck with me. And it would be a long time before I finally figured out what she was talking about.

PHIL AT 6 YEARS OLD.

CHAPTER TWELVE

My first time flying on the C-5A Galaxy after surviving the airplane crash was in June of 1976. I made a decision to marry my girlfriend, Tessie. She was doubtful that I would return to the Philippines because she heard that all GIs say that they will come back for their girlfriends and never do. I was determined to prove her wrong because I really loved her. When I left the Philippines in February of 1976, I promised her that I would return.

The USAF airlifted me back to the States to meet a Medical Evaluation Board. I met the MEB and their findings were to retire me on TDRL (Temporary Disability Retirement List) with a rating of 50 percent. I appealed their decision and won my appeal, and my rating was increased to 60 percent. Two years later my TDRL retirement was made permanent. In the meantime I left Flint Michigan to go get the woman I love.

I went to Selfridge Air Force Base in Mt. Clemens to catch a military hop from Michigan to California. I was excited to try out my new privilege as a retired veteran catching a military hop. I got lucky when I arrived because a slow riding Hercules C-130 was scheduled to leave that same day in route to Travis Air Force Base, California. We didn't have many passengers on board, which was fine with me. After takeoff I told the crew about my Operation Babylift experience and they were in awe because they had heard about the crash.

The aircraft commander invited me to ride up front in the cockpit with the flight crew, which flattered me tremendously. I made my way up to the cockpit happy to leave that dark noisy passenger section.

The pilot and copilot introduced themselves and had me sit in the jump seat, which was right in the middle of the cockpit. I had the most spectacular view looking out at the open skies. The flight was at least seven hours long to Travis and I was able share my story with them in detail. The noise from the engines was very loud but fortunately we were able to communicate through a headset. That was cool. There were times during the flight when I would find myself drifting back to the C-5A Galaxy crash, wondering if the door panel lights would come on and if the latches were secure on this flight. I would hear myself snoring and wake up from my dream and realize that there were no flashing lights.

I often had such nightmares right after the crash. The nightmares got so bad at one point that I would wake up the following morning wet with sweat. I just hoped that I didn't worry the pilots while I was napping. We arrived at Travis AFB in the early afternoon. I thanked the pilots and hugged them both as they wished me well.

That was the first leg of my journey to the Philippines. I was still suffering from the injuries that I sustained in the crash and was hobbling around with some discomfort. I used a walking cane because the pain in my left knee often bothered me. I knew I had a long way to travel with an aching knee reminding me that I wasn't 100 percent healthy. But there was no way I was going to give up on getting back to the P.I. to propose to my girlfriend.

I waited around at Travis AFB Military Airlift Command terminal for a couple of days trying to fly out west toward Asia. Unfortunately, I could not get on a plane out of Travis, and I couldn't afford a commercial flight, so I tried a different route. I'd heard that it was possible to get to Guam by way of San Diego, California. I left my billeting quarters and went to the terminal and saw that a C-5A Galaxy was scheduled to fly into Miramar Naval Air Station later that day. That was great news; I went back to billeting, checked out of my room and returned to the MAC terminal. I signed up for a "space available hop" with plenty of seats open into Miramar Naval Air Station. By the way, all I needed to fly "space" was a retired military ID card.

Take-off was scheduled in a couple of hours and the time was approaching for me to face one of the fears I had pondered since the crash. I wondered if I could fly on the same type of aircraft that I had survived on just over a year before. When it came time to board, a chill hit me as I walked up the stairs to the troop compartment.

Prior to boarding, I had made a decision not to share my C-5A Galaxy experience with the flight crew. I didn't want anybody to know that I survived the crash. Facing my fears and memories was something that I wanted to do alone. I wanted to sit in the seats where the medical crew, flight crew, and the babies sat. The doors closed, the hydraulics roared like before and I paid attention to the latches on the doors. I even asked the load master, "Are you sure the doors are locked?"

"Absolutely," he said.

The engines started and I closed my eyes, thinking of April 4, 1975. I was sitting in the troop compartment and not in the cargo section like before. On the Babylift flight, a majority of us had sat on the cargo floors with blankets spread throughout the section. It was somewhat comforting to sit in the troop compartment knowing that most of the survivors on the C-5A Galaxy crash had been in the troop compartment.

We took off on time and takeoff went smoothly. I thought that the lighting was much better upstairs than downstairs. During the Babylift, the lighting downstairs had been very dim and there was a lot of noise.

On this flight out of California, I sat facing toward the aft (rear) of the aircraft in the front row looking at the flight crew. I tried to imagine what SMSgt. William Parker had gone through during our crash. I turned to my right and located the exit door and the emergency slide near it. SMSgt. Parker had saved many infants through his quick thinking and actions. After the first impact SMSgt. Parker had noticed the inflatable slide inflating. He released his seat belt and took his pocket knife and alertly punched the slide to deflated it and prevented many kids from being injured or killed.

SMSgt. Parker was unable to get back to his seat in time before the second impact. When the airplane hit the second time SMSgt. Parker slid head first down the aisle and slammed into the wall. He was airlifted out of Vietnam to Okinawa where a neurosurgeon would perform emergency surgery. Unfortunately he did not survive his flight there. SMSgt. Parker died a hero for his bravery and actions that saved many lives.

I got up and walked around the galley. I had a look at the stairs that led to the troop compartment. The rear cargo doors were in sight from the galley area. Again, my mind returned to the day of our crash. Our Medical Crew Director (MCD) Lt. Regina Aune had just gone up the stairs right before the doors blew off. Afterwards, she would recall seeing pink hydraulic fluid oozing out from where the doors were.

With the door gone, Lt. Aune saw the South China Sea below as she assisted SMSgt. Perkins up the stairs. SMSgt. Perkins suffered a broken arm as he hung onto a dangling ladder hoping not to fall into the South China Sea. All of these things I'd seen or been told flashed back to me as I was flying just a year after the crash.

When we landed at Miramar Naval Air Station safely, I sought out one of the flight crew members and told him who I was. He immediately told the rest of the crew. Each one of them came over to meet me. The pilot said, "You should have said something. You could have ridden in the flight deck."

I said. "Thanks for the gesture, sir."

My first C-5A Galaxy flight since the crash had gone smoothly; and it helped me avoid my fear of flying on the next C-5A Galaxy.

C-5 A GALAXY
(COURTESY OF LARRY ENGLEMANN AND TONY COALMAN)

JOURNAL ENTRY
MARCH 1975

- *March has arrived and my birthday, March 11ᵗʰ, is coming soon. I have this one flight before my birthday, a mission to Thailand, and boy it is a doozy. We start out that Wednesday leaving Clark with a few passengers and flying dead head to our first stop at Tak Lee Air Base, Thailand. Both flight crew and medical crews are in for a busy day. We have all the stops in Thailand, a full load of patients.*

- *We fly into NKP (Na Kam Phanom), an Army Installation, and pick up a priority patient. This soldier needs special attention. He is strung out on heroin and he has to be sedated and in restraints before boarding. I am flying the third med tech position; so I am responsible for patient care, baggage, enplaning and deplaning of ambulatory and litter patients. Before enplaning our priority patients, it's mandatory to search them because drug patients often try to smuggle drugs when being airlifted to the States.*

- *I board the ambulance and begin my search of our patients. One is named Bro Chi-Chi (not his real name). Bro Chi-Chi is a slim, dark African American soldier. He begins ranting* and loud talking as I plead with him to calm down, but he won't. Finally the flight nurse sedates him with an intramuscular injection of Demerol that immediately knocks him out. Bro. Chi-Chi is on a litter with restraints on his wrists and ankles and straps across his knees and chest.

- Flight number 1541 is now on the way back to Clark Air Base, Philippines, with a full load of patients and no passengers. Our priority patient, Bro Chi-Chi, becomes irrational. I am the only African American crew member on board and it seems like Bro Chi-Chi won't listen to the other crew members. I rush up to him and whisper in his ear and say "Shut the (F) up! We are too high in the sky for you to be showing out like this."

- To my surprise Bro Chi-Chi calms down until his medication wears off. Over and over again during the flight, Bro Chi–Chi falls into episodes of unrest and I am there to help. It seems as though the Demerol didn't have much effect on him. We make our final decent into Clark and Bro Chi-Chi's ranting escalates. Needless to say he is the first to be deplaned once we land.

- Bro Chi-Chi isn't the only drug patient coming out of Thailand; in fact most of our patients are drug abuse patients. Bro Chi-Chi is one of the more severe cases.

- *We normally "RON" (remain overnight) in Utapao or Bangkok, Thailand. Thailand flights are always my favorite trips; I love the Thai food and shopping for gold jewelry, such as rings, bracelets, and earrings.*

- *Guys in the crew often eat and go bar hopping together. The Thai are extremely nice and grateful people. I say that because the Vietnam War is going on and Laos and Cambodia are having their problems as a result of the war. America has multiple bases in Thailand and we are a source of stability for their country's democracy.*

CHAPTER THIRTEEN

I worked odd jobs before I got hired with the US Postal Service in 1984 as a Letter Carrier. My daughter was 5 years old and my boys were teenagers. I was struggling to support my family during those days. I heard that the Post Office was hiring and that veterans had preference. The veteran preference applied to disabled veterans and those with honorable discharge. The veterans preference system awarded fives point to regular veterans and 10 points to disabled veterans when testing for the Postal examination. I was a 10-point vet; therefore I had no trouble passing the postal exam.

I was hired as a part-time flexible carrier (PTF). PTF carriers are not guaranteed 40 hours a week, but we normally worked 40 hours. In order to become a regular carrier one would normally have to work as a PTF for two years, which was the average time it took for a route to become available. My first mail route as a regular carrier was on a rough side of town. The customers were mainly low income people, retired senior citizens and recipients of food stamps and ADC (Aid to Dependent Children).

My customers loved me; they appreciated me because I was very respectful and delivered their mail on time. I enjoyed working in the "hood." I went to work wearing shined shoes, a tie with my uniform, and a great smile. My philosophy was to look professional, well-groomed and to address people as Mr., Mrs. or Miss. That way, most people will respect you. My father drilled that philosophy into me at a very young age, and I maintain it today.

Carrying mail was not without drama. One of my routes held a lot of danger at times. On one occasion, a drive-by shooting went down as I delivered mail on a particular street. I parked my vehicle and grabbed a bundle of mail to carry a swing (a swing is a full street). I delivered mail to the first house on the street and out of nowhere a car came squealing around the corner past me with four guys inside. The guy in the front passenger side seat leaned out the window flailing a shot gun and began pumping rounds at a house in the middle of the block. I got back in my vehicle and surveyed the block only to see that same car come back around again. They slowed down as though they were searching for someone.

It was common knowledge that the street contained numerous drug houses. I skipped that block and came back to it at end of my route and finished my deliveries. Every day it seemed like something was going on along that route. The drama ranged from dog attacks to drug dealing. It got too dangerous for me and I decided to bid off that route.

My next route was slightly better, but it had a history of customers complaining about their checks being stolen. The seniors depended on their Social Security checks on the third of the month and retirement checks on the first of the month. Each month when checks were due out, I made it my duty to personally delivery Social Security and retirement checks to my seniors. I knocked on their doors and placed the checks in their hands.

Anyone who's afraid of dogs should not be a mail carrier. We were raised with dogs in our family, so I was never afraid of dogs. Most dogs have a natural dislike for letter carriers and dog attacks are not uncommon. The Postal Service provided us with a satchel to be used as a shield against dog attacks and dog spray for our protection. I feared something would happen to me sooner or later and then came the incident involving a pit bull.

One house had a young couple with a young kid. Every day when I delivered mail there, the kid would be at the door waving at me. I could hear the dog barking each time. That pit bull was a large, muscular dog and I knew that one day he would come after me. So, I prepared myself for such an attack by putting a wooden club in my satchel, just in case that dog got loose.

One day, a few weeks after I put the club in my satchel, I delivered mail to that house but this time the screen door wasn't closed completely. I had a habit of looking at that house when I parked my jeep. I saw that the front door was open, only the screen door was closed and the kid was not visible. Knowing that the main door was open and the screen door was the only thing that would keep the dog inside, I got worried. I decided to carry the mail on that street anyway but I attached my dog spray to the satchel.

I began my swing at the first house on the same side of the street where the dog lived. After each delivery I took a troubled look at the house to see if the dog was at the door. Midway through my delivery on that block, I saw the kid and the dog at the door. I thought, "Alright, it's time to do battle." Right away, the pit bull charged the door with full force and the door flew wide open. I stopped as the dog charged right toward me. I lifted my satchel off my shoulder and placed it on my arm, grabbed the dog spray repellent in my right hand, and held it in position to spray. The dog spray repellent had a range of 20-30 feet.

I waited until the dog got in range before I released the repellent. The pit bull charged me with speed I hadn't anticipated. I sprayed him, aiming at his eyes and nose, making a direct hit. Homeboy only licked the repellent off and kept charging. I emptied the entire can of dog repellent on him. It had absolutely no effect on that dog, so I quickly reached into my satchel and grabbed my wooden club.

The dog leaped at me and I extended my satchel so he could latch onto it. I began wailing on the pit bull with my wooden club as he locked onto the satchel. I was swinging my satchel around while the dog was locked on it, and at the same time I was hitting him and hitting him. Finally, a lady from across the street came outside her house and called the dog off me. He released his grip from my satchel and ran into the lady's home. Never had I been so happy to have a satchel on my arm and a wooden club in my hand.

Working as a letter carrier took a toll on my knee. Many days I worked in absolute pain. I decided to try management so I come off the streets. That helped for a while until management decided to send me back out as a carrier. I was hoping to make it in management but was never promoted.

The Flint Post Office did not necessarily promote people to management who had people skills. Instead, some managers had been lousy carriers with lousy work records but reached a position to give orders to other carriers. That was the essence of so many disgruntled carriers going "postal."

I continued working as a carrier, but the pain became so severe that it was difficult for me to walk and I could not bear it any longer. I went to my supervisor and ask to work inside the office. My work record was impeccable. I had only missed one day of work in 12 years. Instead of helping me transition to an inside job, management decided to boot me out of the Postal Service. I was processed out on disability retirement, with the Postal Service claiming that no other positions were available.

The only recourse I had was to file for Workman's Compensation. I hired an attorney to represent me; my union was limited in terms of helping me. It was rare for any lawyer to take on the Postal Service, but my attorney accepted the case and was able to prove that my service-related injury was aggravated by my position as a letter carrier. I won my case and the Postal Service was forced to design a job for me to work inside. I eventually rejected each job proposal they offered me, because I was convinced that management would constantly harass me.

After I refused all the job offers, Workman's Compensation stopped paying me. I was forced to go back to receiving disability retirement. I was fine with that decision, because the way I was treated by the Postal Service was unacceptable. I was a loyal employee who was disrespected, and my honor was attacked. I was a disabled veteran who worked very hard for 12 years and missed only one day of work. I've received many awards and letters of appreciation during my career and none of that mattered.

Fortunately for me I saved my sick leave. I saved more than 1,300 sick leave hours and more than 400 annual leave hours. Those hours came in handy while I battled with the Postal Service to win my Workman's Compensation case. My pay was regularly short on hours. Sometimes my supervisors computed my sick leave hours inaccurately and that meant I could not meet my financial obligations. I'm not sure if that was deliberate, but it created hardship for my family.

I miss my Postal Service customers, the love they showed me; the Christmas cards and gifts and representing the Postal Service. That was my life! It's a shame I had to leave my job that way.

FAMILY PHOTO, 1978

CHAPTER FOURTEEN

Twenty-five years had gone by since the C-5A Galaxy crash and I found myself eager to locate any of the surviving crew members. It wasn't until 2005 when I was able to establish contact with the pilot, Aircraft Commander Dennis "Bud" Traynor. I found Bud during the time I caught a military hop to the Philippines in February 2000. My wife's mom, who lived with us at the time, passed away. Tessie flew her mom's body back to the Philippines for burial service. That was her mom's final request before she died, to be buried at home in the Philippines. They flew back commercially.

I decided to fly by way of military space available. I called Selfridge Air National Base operations. Fortunately they had a flight coming in the first of the week. To my surprise I was told that a C-5A Galaxy would arrive Monday heading to Travis AFB, California. I signed up for the flight and had my friend Pete Nichols drop me off at the base. A couple of passengers had signed up for the same flight. I went into base operation and showed my identification and got my seat reservation. The base operation officer told me that it was rare for a C-5A Galaxy to land at Selfridge.

While I was in base ops I could see a large aircraft positioned outside, a huge black and green camouflage airplane sitting all alone. As I was staring at it, a pilot came inside the building and went to base operation to file his flight plan. I stopped him and asked, "Are you the pilot of that C-5A parked outside?"

"Yes," he said.

I introduced myself and told him that I was a crew member on board the C-5A Galaxy that crashed during Operation Babylift, April 4, 1975, and asked him, "Do you know Bud Traynor?"

He replied, "Bud Traynor? Why heck yeah, everybody knows Bud Traynor! He is one of our heroes."

I was elated to hear that news. I told the Major that I had been searching for Bud for many years. From that point on I was given the

VIP treatment. The whole flight team came and introduced themselves. I was invited ride in the flight deck all the way to Travis.

What surprised me was how shocked they were to learn that I survived in the cargo section. They all thought that there were no survivors on the bottom of the aircraft. Naturally they wanted to hear my story and learn about what went on downstairs. Some of the flight crew knew some of my crew members who died on that flight. They hung on my every word when I told my story. I had with me some newspaper articles and photos of me receiving the Airmen's Medal. I really felt good about the attention I was getting because prior to that I hadn't talked much about the crash. The AC (aircraft commander) requested me to come and ride in the jump seat, which is right up front in the cockpit. That was awesome. He wanted me to tell him and the copilot all about the Operation Babylift. Of course I was more than happy tell my story again.

The flight deck is like sitting in an office. It has a table that is mounted to the floor with comfortable seats that stretch along the side of the aircraft. Another table on the other side has seats along the wall. The plane has sleeping quarters with curtains for privacy during crew rest, and a lavatory and shower. I was given a tour of the entire aircraft by one of the load masters. I felt like a celebrity, especially when other passengers saw me getting the VIP treatment.

The ride in the flight deck and cockpit was extremely smooth and quiet. We were cruising at an altitude of 35,000 feet with clear skies. The view from the cockpit looking at the sky was breathtaking, unlike riding in the dim troop compartment with a couple of windows to look out. Our flight time to Travis was about five hours. We made it to our destination and deplaned. I got my luggage and went to the MAC terminal to sign up for the next leg of my journey. The pilot knew I was trying to get to the Philippines and called ahead and told me that another C-5A Galaxy was taking off shortly heading to Anderson AFB, Guam, with plenty of seats available.

When I went to the terminal, I saw this same pilot walking with a two-star General. He called me over and introduced us, and said he'd told Major General Whaley all about me. General Whaley asked me to walk with him to the aircraft and once again I was invited to ride in the flight deck. On the way to Guam, I sat at the same table as the General who eagerly asked to hear my story. I told him the whole story and I let him know that I was searching for the pilot of the C-5A Galaxy. I explained that I had not seen my friend, the pilot, since he visited me in the hospital at Clark AFB, Philippines, in April 1975.

General Whaley cheerfully said to me, "I know Bud Traynor. He and wife Pam run our AT/A conventions."

A look of utter joy came across my face when I heard that news. I said to the General, "Faith has brought us together to help me in my search for Bud Traynor."

DENNIS BUD TRAYNOR AND PHIL WISE ABOARD
WORLD AIRWAY'S
HOMEWARD BOUND REUNIFICATION FLIGHT
BACK TO VIETNAM, 2005

JOURNAL ENTRY
APRIL 1, 1975

April begins with an off day and I spend time with Tessie. We take in a movie at one of our favorite theaters in downtown, Angeles City. Anytime there is a new Bruce Lee movie out we go to see it. Enter the Dragon is his latest. We go to Manila the next day to visit her cousin Dael and do some shopping. I know if I don't spend time with her now it will not happen for a while. April third is a work day and I have standby duty. The duty hours start at 0700 thru 0700 the next morning. We arrive back at Angeles City later that evening and I stay the night at my apartment. It's 0600 hours April 3, 1975, and I wake up ready to get back to the base. Curfew is over at 0600 hours and the main gate is open. I ride a jeepney to check point and go through the main gate and catch the shuttle bus to my barrack. My room is sparkling clean; Eddy has hooked me up. I take a shower and go to the chow hall and have breakfast. Afterward I go to the squadron and pick up my radio to start duty at 0700 hours.

- *I grab my radio from the squadron and check my schedule. I have an upcoming flight to Taiwan, which is cool because I can shop for jade on that trip. After taking care of business*

I head back off base. Alert crews on standby must be near a phone and carry a radio with them at all times.

- *Fortunately there is no action the entire day and evening. I stay at the apartment most of the day. Tessie brings by food that she prepared and we have dinner. We relax for a while and I go back to the base early. It is about 1900 hours (7:00 pm) when I get back to the barracks. The Airman's Club on base is a jumping place, so I decide to go there and hang out. I have a couple of beers, play pool and watch everybody dance. It is getting late and I am tired, so I go back to the barracks to crash. Normally if you make it past 2300 hours without being alerted to fly, chances are you aren't going to fly that night.*

- *I go to bed as soon as I make it back to the barracks. I am resting well and then I hear a loud knock on my door. The pounding from the knock echoes. I think I am dreaming, then I jump up and answer the door. It is the CQ (charge of quarters) alerting me that squadron called; the time is 0655 hours. The CQ says "You've been alerted to fly." I think for a minute, and say "Maybe I should call the squadron, because I am off duty in five more minutes and maybe they are mistaken."*

CHAPTER FIFTEEN

It was April 30, 2007 when I finally got an interview with Retired Col. Tilford Harp. I've been waiting for years to talk to him. In the year 2000, I briefly spoke with him over the phone. I tracked him down at Altus A.F.B., OK. He was one of the C-5A Galaxy instructors. At the time he could not talk in any details about the crash because he had to work. But he did put me in contact with Bud Traynor. Thanks to Major General Whaley for information that allowed me to find Tilford. Now it's 2007, and I've reconnected with Tilford Harp. This time he's in San Antonio, Texas, working again as a flight instructor. I asked him what, if anything, he remembered about me and my rescue. I was desperate to find out anything about my rescue. Unfortunately he knew nothing.

He said, "I was trapped in the wreckage struggling to get loose."

The C-5A Galaxy had come down fast. It was pretty clear the aircraft was not going to make it back to Tan Son Nhut Air Base when trouble hit. Tilford strapped himself and prepared for a crash landing. The aircraft clipped some low lying trees before it touched down the first time. Tilford braced himself for the second impact. He was not sure if we would clear the Saigon River after the aircraft went airborne again; fortunately we made it across, barely.

The aircraft touched down again, but this time more violently, causing the cockpit to break apart and roll over to its side. When the aircraft came to a complete stop, Tilford found himself hanging upside down. He said, "I struggled to get free, but had a lot of difficulty." He managed to reverse his position and dangle his legs trying once more to get free, only to find that he had two broken ankles.

Tilford recalled seeing many helicopters lined up evacuating babies concentrated near the troop compartment. He recalled seeing tons of wreckage being looted and immediately taken away by the villagers. It was very painful for Tilford to bring up the memories of the crash and talk about it. I didn't press him; I just asked if he remembered seeing me during the rescue at all.

He said he only remembered seeing so many helicopters taking so many folks away; he had no idea who was who.

Colonel Tilford Harp is a hero. He demonstrated exceptional skills that day. Colonel Harp received the USAF Distinguished Flying Cross for gallantry and bravery.

WRECKAGE AT CRASH SITE 1975

COURTESY OF LARRY ENGLEMANN/TONY COALMAN

CHAPTER SIXTEEN

Denning Cicero (DC) Johnson was born into a poor family, one of five boys. His father was blind and died when DC was 16. The military seemed to him to be his best option, and he joined at age 17. He was a travel and flying enthusiast, so when he turned 18, hoping to capitalize on these interests, he joined the Air Force. As an enlisted man, he wasn't able to be a pilot; and since to him the next best thing was to be on the planes, he became an airborne medic, serving on flights all over Asia. He was a dedicated family man, and he took his wife and children with him wherever he was stationed.

DC wasn't supposed to be on the C5-A but got assigned as a last minute switch; so even when his family and friends heard about the crash they weren't worried about him. By the afternoon of the 4th they knew he was involved, but it wasn't until 0700 the next morning that they were told the terrible news that he had been killed. Two weeks later they were the recipients of a closed casket and very few personal effects. So for 30 some years they wondered – why did it take so long to get his body and was it really him? Had he actually been on that plane? And if he was, what was the truth surrounding his death?

I have visited the wall on many of the anniversaries of the crash, just about every five years. In 2005 I went with Marci Wirtz Tate, a flight nurse who was also on that flight. That was the year I met DC's children, his son Harry, who was 8 years old at the time of his father's death, and Denise, who was age 15 when DC died.

Denise had visited the wall many times, and she always found it extremely moving. She said, "You just don't realize how just seeing a name on a monument can affect you like this one can."

She was once there with her 8-year-old nephew, named for her father. They were looking at the wall, and when they finally got to DC's panel, the boy could not see the name. The nephew did not seem to mind, saying, "He's just a name to me." For Denise, that was devastating. Two years later they were passing the North Carolina Vietnam Memorial and he asked to stop. That time he saw things differently, and said how proud he was to see his grandfather's name there. Denise said she looked forward to bringing him back to the memorial in Washington.

I told Denise and Harry that I was the one who had been mentored by DC and had survived the C5-A crash. It was an emotional meeting, but it enlightened DC's children and eased their feelings of uncertainty. It put to rest more than 30 years of wondering what had happened.

I filled in some of the gaps for DC's children:

DC and I worked together in the Philippines. I was much younger, and DC helped to train me. DC was a wonderful person and a real hero. We were among the medical technicians who ran in-flight hospitals all over Asia.

On April 4, 1975 we were serving together in Vietnam on the first Operation Babylift flight out of Saigon. I assigned both of us to the cargo section in the underbelly of the plane. As the plane began to climb we spent our time assisting patients, mostly hysterical children who had never been in a plane before and didn't understand where they were going or what was happening to them.

It would later be determined that the C5-A had faulty locks in the rear cargo doors that blew off when the plane reached about 25,000 feet. The casualties were enormous in our section; in fact, for years I thought I was the only person to survive, but learned later that a child was also spared, although suffering terrible injuries. I woke up two days later in the intensive care unit in the Philippines.

I didn't tell DC's children about the frightening dreams I have had for years after the crash. The images come back like fuzzy, fog-filled memories and stories told to me that blend into nightmares. In the dreams, I see the sharp light, the gaping hole, the blinding sky. Confused, I wobble, horror-struck, simultaneously grasping for something to hold onto and reaching out toward babies and adults whose screams fill my ears. The terrified children are ripped from the floor and out into the air in a forceful pull, unable to hold onto anything. They disappear by the dozens in a sudden and unimaginable few seconds as the pilot tries to land the plane. And I see a good friend hanging on the stair trying to make it upstairs. And all goes black for me as I tumble into falling wires. Once awake, my memories remain clouded. I think I must have buried the horror so deeply that I cannot clearly remember all that I saw before I blacked out. And nothing again until I wake up in the hospital at Clark AFB.

On the 20th anniversary of the crash I was at the wall with my young daughter, and she took a photo of me pointing to the names of our comrades, who are all grouped together based on the date of their deaths. Later she showed me the picture that seems to show an angel sitting above my shoulder.

VISIT TO THE VIETNAM VETERAN MEMORIAL WALL ON APRIL 4, 1995 WHERE AN IMAGE OF AN ANGEL APPEARS OVER MY SHOULDER

JOURNAL ENTRY

APRIL 3, 1975 (continued)

- So, now it's after 0700 hours and nothing is on the flight line ready to go. I'm a little mad at this point and go into the squadron office to find out what's going on. I speak with TSgt. Turner Smith in the control room who calmly says, "Be patient, Sgt. Wise. And don't go anywhere." An hour passes and I go back to the control center for information and this time Sgt. Turner's demeanor is different. He says, "The Aircraft Commander and Wing Commander will call a briefing shortly, so just hang around."

- Three hours pass. Finally the briefing is called and all crew members are present. The Wing Commander starts the briefing by explaining the dire situation in Saigon with enemy forces merging on the outskirts. He talks about the many orphanages trying to move children into Saigon and how many Amer-Asian babies are trapped in the transition of warring governments. He talks about how the government fears those kids will be persecuted if left behind. He announces the name of our mission and calls it

Operation Babylift by order of the President of the United States, Gerald R. Ford.

- Suddenly it all starts to make sense -- the secrecy, the urgency and the assembly of two medical crews. This is highly unusual. The most surprising thing is the announcement of using the C5-A Galaxy to airlift these kids. Our mission is to fly to Saigon, South Vietnam, and start the evacuation of more than 2,000 babies.

- Our medical crews have never flown on a C5-A Galaxy, so we have to take a quick walk-through of the aircraft and learn what we can in terms of configuration to aero medical evacuation.

- I walk outside our building using the rear exit onto the flight line. I see the huge C5-A Galaxy, and I just stare at it. The rear doors are opened and the ramp's down, the nose is lifted and I can see all the way through it. On the walk-through, the load master used his check list to point out safety features and emergency exits throughout the aircraft. We see several howitzers tied down on the cargo floor. I'm thinking this cargo must be for the South Vietnamese government and it must be a serious situation in Vietnam.

CHAPTER SEVENTEEN

My wife, Tessie and I wanted to do something special for the 30th anniversary of the C-5A Galaxy crash. My wife made a beautiful wreath to be placed at the Vietnam Veterans Memorial Wall on April 4, 2005. The wreath ceremony was to recognize the loss of 11 crew members during Operation Babylift's humanitarian evacuation mission.

During the same time the New Jersey Vietnam Veterans Memorial Foundation honoring the 30th anniversary of Operation Babylift. I was invited as one of the guest speakers. My wife and I made plans to attend both events. We traveled to the New Jersey event first and then headed to Washington, DC for the wreath laying ceremony.

On April 2, 2005 I took part in the New Jersey Vietnam Veterans Memorial and Vietnam-era Educational Center's 30th Anniversary of Operation Babylift. A diverse group of speakers participated in the program. One was Jennifer Nguyen Noone, a Babylift adoptee who was once interviewed by People Magazine, Newsday and USA Today. Jennifer's adoptive mother Lana Noone, a classical flutist, performed traditional Vietnamese songs. Lana and her late husband, Byron, adopted two Operation Babylift children (Jennifer and Heather) and a child from Korea (Jason). Heather was sick when she arrived from the orphanage in Vietnam and died her first year in America.

LeAnn Thieman, an accomplished author and a dynamic speaker who helped transport more than 300 babies from Vietnam to America during Operation Babylift, also attended. LeAnn contributed money, time and love by adopting children. Her book, "This Must Be My Brother," has been featured in Newsweek magazine, Fox-TV News and on PAX-TV's "It's A Miracle" show. LeAnn, Lana Noone, five other authors and I are in negotiations with

Hollywood for a feature film, "It's 110 Degrees in Saigon and Getting Hotter."

Jared Rehberg, an accomplished guitarist and a Babylift adoptee, performed songs from his hit CD "Waking Up American." Jared was adopted into a great family from New York. He heard my presentation and was very touched by my story. Jared was one of the adoptees invited to travel to Vietnam with the World Airways Homeward Bound Unification flight to honor the 30th anniversary. Each adoptee was able to bring a guest. To my surprise Jared invited me to join him as his guest on the trip.

I was thrilled to be a part of the World Airways historic reunification flight to Vietnam. Unfortunately my wife was not allowed to travel with me. She graciously understood and encouraged me to make the trip. After the New Jersey event my wife and I made our way down interstate 95 heading to Washington, DC.

My dear friend Marcia Wirtz Tate and husband Marty traveled from Virginia to take part in the ceremony at the Vietnam Veterans Memorial Wall. Marcie was one of the flight nurses that survived in the troop compartment upstairs. Her heroics saved the lives of many babies. She told her story in the Reflections of Flight Nursing magazine:

"I was on one of my bottle-filling jaunts to the galley 20 minutes or so after take-off when disaster struck. The huge rear cargo doors through which our delicate passengers had just enplaned blew off. With it went control mechanisms and part of the cargo section. A tremendous boom shook the plane. 'It just can't be a rapid decompression,' I told myself in disbelief! But one look down and the sight of a massive hole in the monstrous C-5A Galaxy, revealing the bright blue South China Sea far below, made the truth starkly clear.

"Shock and fear must have been quite evident on each of our faces as we quickly prepared for what our hearts and minds told us would be a 'touchy' if not 'terminal' landing. We piled pillows between the babies for more padding, and each of us took a well learned 'crash position' as we prepared for the inevitable.

"I was on my knees between two seats and with my arms extended over four children. I tucked my head into their laps and prayed. 'Our father, who art in Heaven...' Suddenly, I felt the plane bounce as it did at least three times before this section exploded."

Aero Medical Evacuation Association sponsored the wreath laying ceremony with my good friend CMSgt. Wayne Everingham (Secretary of AMEA). Also in attendance was my best friend Reverend Jim Harden (Major USAF, Retired); Cletus Bell (CMSgt. USAF, Retired); Claudia Bell (Lt. Col. USAF) and a host of active duty personnel. We had two special guests in attendance, Denise and Harry Johnson, the kids of my fallen crewmember Denning C. Johnson.

At the ceremony they met both Marcie, but my wife and I had had dinner with Denise and Harry the night before where they learned the details of my story. I let them know that their dad was a real hero and that he did not suffer because when the doors blew off our oxygen left the cabin instantly and we passed out before we hit the ground.

Denise, Harry and I were very emotional talking about C-5A the Galaxy crash, with tears were rolling down our cheeks. I was touched by their persistence to find out what happened to their dad. They brought with them newspaper articles about Operation Babylift but nothing in the articles had satisfied their search for answers on what happened to DC Johnson.

Denise and Harry thanked me for coming to Washington, DC to honor the C-5A Galaxy crew and especially their dad. Before placing the wreath at the wall, Marcie and I spoke to the crowd who had gathered there. We both read the names of our fallen crew members and told a little bit about each. We recognized all of our distinguished guests before we placed the wreath at the Vietnam Veterans Memorial Wall.

After we laid the wreath, the wind picked up and blew strongly. Everyone looked up and we noticed a beautiful golden brown speckled butterfly flying above us. The butterfly danced around and hovered over us, and suddenly it descended toward me. I was standing across from where the wreath was placed and the butterfly landed on my left hand and stayed there. Everybody was marveling over this butterfly landing on my hand. People were snapping pictures and surrounding me trying to get a closer look at this amazing butterfly.

My good friend Reverend Jim Harden was standing next to me and thought he would get in on the action. He thought maybe he could lure this butterfly from my hand to his hand. I had my forefinger extended, sort of in a pointing position. Rev. placed his forefinger in front of mine hoping that the butterfly would walk across to his finger. The butterfly was facing Rev. but once Rev. nosed his finger up to mine, the butterfly did an about-face and flapped his wings indicating to Rev. to "Get back, I'm here for Phil!" Everybody started laughing and Rev. threw his hands up in the air and said, "Ok, I'm out of here."

In the meantime my wife used my video camera to capture the butterfly on my hand. Two or three minutes had passed by the time she started filming and the butterfly stayed on my hand. The film was rolling and my wife captured all that was going on surrounding the butterfly. Suddenly the wind picked up again and blew the wreath over onto the ground. The butterfly left my hand and flew down to park itself right next to the wreath. It was amazing!

The butterfly stayed on the ground for a long while. I went over to Denise and Harry and told them that this butterfly appearing here with us at the wall must be a sign from our crew members letting us know that they approve of what we are doing here today, April 4, 2005. Thirty years later a blessing appeared at the wall.

A BUTTERFLY VISITS ME DURING A CEREMONY ON APRIL 4, 2005, HONORING FALLEN CREW MEMBERS FROM OPERATION BABYLIFT C-5A GALAXY CRASH.

CHAPTER EIGHTEEN

In early May 2011, I received a call from Sister Susan who wanted to know if I was coming to St. Louis for a Babylift reunion at her place. The reunion was scheduled for late May and Babylift adoptees from around the country and two from Switzerland were to attend. Sister Mary Gage Nelle would be there as Sister Susan's special guest. She helped place many adoptees into loving homes all over the world and had worked with Sister Susan at an orphanage in Vietnam.

Sister Mary Gage Nelle wanted to meet me; we spoke briefly over the phone during my conversation with Sister Susan. I assured her that I would make the reunion in St. Louis. My wife and daughter signed on to come along with me. I wanted my family to meet the Babylift families I've been connected to for many years. Sister Susan and I have been friends for a long time but my wife and daughter had never met her.

My family and I took a fun and exciting drive to St. Louis, Missouri from Flint, Michigan. We talked about what to expect once we arrived, and we were not disappointed when we got there.

First, we attended a get-acquainted or meet-and-greet time at Sister Susan's house with plenty of food and drinks. Afterwards, a group of us went into downtown St. Louis to a local grill where we had dinner and drinks. We were getting to know each other and had much fun doing so, taking photos and keeping up a steady stream of conversations, questions and curiosity -- especially from the Operation Babylift adoptees. Many had a deep thirst for any information about the Babylift and I was there for them. Just like Sister Susan said during our phone conversation, "Phil, the kids will have a lot of questions for you."

These kids/adoptees loved Sister Susan and I understand why. Sister Susan was in the trenches back in the day. She gave up so much of her young life to protect so many kids that were trapped in the orphanages. Sister Susan knew what orphanage many of the children came from in Vietnam. She had a treasure chest full of photos in her library.

I remember when Sister Susan introduced Sister Mary Gage Nelle to me and my family. I'd been hoping for such a meeting long before we talked on the phone. I'd heard about the many orphanages Sister Mary cared for and supervised.

Sister Susan shared with Sister Mary how she found me clinging to life once I entered the emergency room after the crash. Sister Susan was a nurse volunteering at the Seventh Day Adventist hospital when the C-5A Galaxy went down.

She said she saw me when I was brought into the emergency room and was afraid I was not going to make it. She prayed for me as the trauma team worked on me. My white shirt was drenched in blood while I was lying on the stretcher. She prayed again for me and stayed near my side while I was treated.

Sister Susan is very affectionate and still shows that same affection today with the kids. The adoptees brought gifts for Sister Susan and we collected donations to help replenish the money she spent for the reunion. Her friend Mary Louis was great. She did a wonderful job accommodating everyone at their home. She had her chef's hat on while roasting the pig. We had all kinds of side dishes to munch on. The adoptees loved having Pho on the menu (a popular Vietnamese soup).

That night I met Shane Dewey and Jimmy Zimmerly, who survived as kids in the troop compartment section of the plane. We embraced and hugged each other with so much love and feeling, it was as though we had met before -- and in a sense we had met before. I also met Jimmy's adopted mother, Wanda Zimmerly, a sweetheart and truly precious person. She gave me a videotape of a 20/20 interview I was on in 1984. I had been looking for that interview for a long time and Wanda came through for me.

Saturday's schedule included indulging on that succulent roasted pig we had been waiting to eat. We went to the St. Louis Zoo and a few people attended a St. Louis Cardinals game. My wife, my daughter and I stayed at the house with Sister Susan. The youngsters went out to explore St. Louis while the more senior guests stayed back.

That gave me more time to talk with Wanda Zimmerly. I remembered her from the 2010 trip to Vietnam but really didn't get a chance to talk with her then. That trip had been for the 35th anniversary of OBL (Operation Babylift) April 4, 2010. We had organized the trip through Facebook. Babylift kids from all over the world made the trip. Well more than 80 people showed up.

I told Wanda that I remembered her from last year's trip to Vietnam and she remembered me, too! In Vietnam she didn't know my story; she only remembered we had met at the market in District One, Ho Chi Minh City (formally Saigon). The market place was the rendezvous spot. From there we walked to the restaurant as a group.

A weird thing happened on the way to the restaurant. We were standing at the cross walk waiting for the light to change. When the light changed, as we crossed the street I was in the back of the group. The street was very wide and when the light changed back I hadn't crossed the street entirely. The cars began to move across the intersection and I noticed a motor bike coming toward me as I neared the sidewalk. I was caring my camera bag with me and began to grip it tightly. I don't know but something told me to keep an eye on that motor bike. The guy on the bike made a sudden turn right at me and tried to grab my camera bag. He grabbed it, but I yanked back my bag and he almost fell off his bike. He regained his balance and looked at me and then took off really fast.

Everyone in our group kept walking and did not know what was going on. After fighting off the biker thief I ran to catch up with the group. That ordeal reminded me of how dangerous it is for tourists in Saigon, and it reminded me of the time my watch got snatched off my arm as I rode a jeepney in the Philippines a long time ago. We made it to the restaurant in time for the 7 p.m. dinner gala.

The restaurant was fabulous and full of customers. We had more than 80 people in our group alone. We gathered in a private section of the restaurant and had great service. Sister Susan invited me to sit at her table with Safi Dubb and her family. Safi and I had met 10 years earlier on the Internet. We finally got a chance to meet in person. It was wonderful meeting Safi. We hugged and pulled back to look at each other, then hugged more and cried together. Safi survived the C-5A Galaxy crash, too. She was only six weeks old the day we evacuated her out of Saigon, secured in one of the seats upstairs in the troop compartment.

Safi introduced me to six other survivors who were at the table. We shared individual stories about ourselves and family. They wanted me to describe what went on during that fatal time on the airplane. I was happy to share with them my recollection of the events of that day. They listened to me intently as I described the horror that went on downstairs in the troop compartment. After I spoke, Benoit Thorel, Emma McCrudden, Annabelle Bommelaere, Safi Dubb, and Joakim Kim Kronqvist gave me big hugs. We cried, we laughed, we held hands, and we embraced one another some more.

I choked up when all of them thanked my fallen crew members for their sacrifices. I was overwhelmed by that unexpected showing of love for my fallen crew members. It touched my heart and I found myself wiping my eyes and fighting back sobs. It was beautiful! We were asked to take photos together and dozens of people started snapping our pictures. We really drew a lot of attention.

After dinner we went out to a nearby disco where we partied until the early morning hours. My good friend Joakim took good care of me. He made sure I got back to my hotel room safely. I was pretty lit up and I really appreciated his concern for my safety, especially after the near theft of my camera earlier.

The next day was a big day for us. Sister Susan had organized a tour to the crash site for the memorial service. My hotel was a block away from the one where we were to depart. That lobby was full of people and many I knew came up to me. We took pictures and talked about how exciting it was to be in Vietnam.

We spent a lot of time talking about the crash site. It would be the first time back for many of them. The religious belief for some in Vietnam is that the souls won't rest until a memorial marker is in place near the crash site grounds. A lot of the conversation took place about how we could get land reserved near the site for a memorial dedication. I understood that it would take going through a lot of red tape and politics.

Many Vietnamese believe that America stole their kids during the Babylift. I think that's ridiculous, because I could see how the Amer-Asian adults were treated in Ho Chi Minh City -- as third class citizens. I looked at them and wondered if they wanted to know about their fathers.

Putting a memorial dedication at the crash site remains a hot button issue. We arrived in the area and walked along the dusty dirt road that led to the crash site. Well over 100 people joined us. Sister Susan and her friends who worked at her orphanage passed out incense to light for the Buddhist rite: We all received sticks of burning incense and bags with candies, cookies, paper garments and paper toys for children, and food, plates and more for offerings to the spirits of those who died here.

We formed a circle and each of us read the names of each loved person including my crew members. After the reading, we tossed bags of cookies, candies, and treats into the air. These symbolize giving gifts of happiness to the children who died in the crash. The treats left behind were collected and enjoyed by children who live in the area. Sister Susan read this quote, "In our hearts, we acknowledge with love each of these individuals. You may presume these people are here, present with us now. We give them our love and receive love from them."

Everyone received a copy of a poem by a Vietnamese poet, Thich Nhat Hanh. We sang in the spirit of Kum Ba Yah, "This Is Holy Ground, Kum Ba Yah," lead by Sister Susan. We concluded by singing, "There are angels here, Kum Ba Yah - We remember you, Kum Ba Yah, - We're together here - Kum Ba Yah, - Precious loved ones - Kum Ba Ya."

Memories of that visit to Vietnam came back at the reunion in St Louis. Sister Susan is clearly a gift from God. She has touched the lives of so many people including my own. It was magical watching her educating the kids about the orphanages in Vietnam. I don't know how she knew the names of so many adoptees and who took care of them when they were in the orphanages. Sister Susan Carol MacDonald is my friend and hero. She went above and beyond the call of duty during and after the Vietnam War in taking care of the kids of war. I believe her leadership and prayers have saved many, many lives. That's what makes her an American hero.

SISTER SUSAN MACDONALD AND PHIL WISE STANDING BEHIND A MAKESHIFT MEMORIAL MADE FROM WRECKAGE OF A C5-A GALAXY PART LOCATED IN 2006 IN A VILLAGE NEAR THE CRASH SITE.

JOURNAL ENTRY
APRIL 4, 1975

- *Lieutenant Regina Aune is in charge of our medical team as the medical crew director (MCD). Regina comes from the 10th Aerovac Travis AFB, California along with James A. Hadley, Michael C. Paget, and Mary T. Klinker. As senior medical technician (SMT), I am in charge of all the medical technicians. My job is to designate my second medical technician and the third med tech to perform specific duties and work in different sections of the aircraft.*

- *I assign Denning C. Johnson, Michael C. Pagett and myself to work the cargo section and Gregory Gmerek, James A. Hadley, and Olen Boutwell to work the troop compartment (upper level passengers' seats). Regina assigns Mary Klinker to help us in the cargo section and assigns Marcia Wirtz and Harriet Goffinet to work in the troop compartment. Each of the med techs is assigned to work with the nurses. We have no idea what to expect in terms of patient care and needs when we get to Vietnam. Captain Dennis Bud Traynor is our aircraft commander (pilot). He closes the aircraft as we prepare for take-off. We take off at* approximately 1030hrs Pacific Standard Time headed to Tan Son Nhut Air Force Base, South Vietnam.

- The flight crew and the medical crews ride in the flight deck in route to Vietnam. We laugh and talk on the way there. Some of us have questions about the situation on the ground, such as is it safe, or will it be chaos on base, or will we encounter enemy fire? All we know is Saigon is about to fall and the communist regime is closing in on the capital city.

- Captain Traynor starts his descent into Tan Son Nhut Air Base and we strap ourselves in for landing. We touch down a little after 1200 hours. The aircraft comes to a complete stop in an area far off the flight line.

- One by one the buses are unloaded and the kids are enplaned. We start with the infants and load them upstairs in the troop compartment. We form a chain line and pass each child up the ladder to be placed in the seats, two babies per seat. They are as young as 2 years old and younger. It is so hot and my uniform is soaked and wet from perspiration. The stench from the odor of soiled diapers just as quickly engulfs the entire cabin. The odor almost becomes unbearable to the crew.

- *We are helped with loading the kids by a volunteer group called "Friends of Children of Vietnam" (FCVN) ;they are familiar with some of the kids and orphanages that they come from. They are great with the kids and they help with loading them in the cargo hold section. They care for many of the frightened toddlers who are lost in their surroundings wondering what is going on. I notice photographers filming and taking pictures capturing all that is going on inside the aircraft.*

- *Other organizations also are helping with the evacuation of Operation Babylift orphans. The women from the DAO, (Defense Attaché Office) are instrumental in organizing and providing documents for those orphans leaving. Two hours pass and we are ready for takeoff. We use cargo tie-down straps across our laps to secure everybody in place for takeoff. The adults sit on the cargo floor. The older kids sit alongside the cat walk.*

CHAPTER NINETEEN

Rose Mary Taylor, a nurse from Australia who founded several orphanages in Vietnam, decided not to put the children in her care on a World Airways aircraft because she had heard it was not safe for transporting the children.

The US government didn't want any more unauthorized Babylift flights leaving Vietnam coming to the USA, so the President launched Operation Babylift and Rose Mary chose to put her children on that first flight to Tan Son Nhut Air Base..

I met with Rosemary Taylor in Washington DC in 1982 when I was testifying on behalf of the defense team representing the kids in a lawsuit. Rosemary was there testifying, too. She heard about me surviving the C-5A Galaxy crash and was excited to talk with me. I learned that she was very torn up about her decision to put that group of kids on the C-5A Galaxy and not on the World Airways flight. She was upset that she lost close friends who worked with her at the Phu My orphanage. Rosemary was from Australia and had recruited several women from the US and other parts of the world to help with orphanages in Vietnam.

She held my hand and told how special her friends were who worked for her at the orphanage. She asked me if I remembered seeing Margaret Moses from her orphanage or from the DAO. I could not answer to seeing any particular individual, because all the volunteers were new faces to me. The only thing I could do was describe what went on downstairs. I was able to give her comfort by sharing with her how the rapid decompression caused me to pass out before the crash landing. She realized that many of her friends did not suffer on impact like she thought.

For many years I thought the C-5A Galaxy was the first Operation Babylift flight until I went to court and talked with Rosemary Taylor. Little did I know that my life would be intertwined with these orphans and changed forever. The US government vilified Ed Daly for airlifting the orphans out of Vietnam without authorization, but to many he was a hero. He got the ball rolling and forced the government to make a decision to launch the largest evacuation of kids in US history. Thanks to Ed Daly many of the Operation Babylift kids are living in freedom in many parts of the world.

I am proud to be a part of that history. I'm blessed the good Lord spared my life on April 4, 1975. My story is only a small part of the Babylift story. Some of the kids I've met have great stories to tell; and most of all they are truly grateful for their freedom.

PHIL, PAM AND BUD TRAYNOR STANDING IN FRONT OF WORLD AIRWAYS' MD-11 AIRCRAFT BEFORE BOARDING ON HOMEWARD BOUND FLIGHT TO VIETNAM, JUNE 2005

CHAPTER TWENTY

The Internet gave me an avenue to connect with my Babylift people. In 2001 I came in contact with one of the first Operation Babylift kids who survived the C-5A Galaxy crash, thanks to Sister Susan Carol MacDonald. After I connected with Sister Susan on the Internet she put me in touch with a young lady named Safi Thi-Kim Felce. Sister Susan told me Safi wanted my e-mail address and wanted to be in touch with me. Naturally I agreed. I was excited about getting a chance to meet my first Babylift kid 26 years after the crash. I had often wondered what had become of the Babylift kids.

Sister Susan told Safi all about me, and Safi was just as excited to talk to me as I was to hear from her. Safi sent me an e-mail that read:

"I got your e-mail address from Sister Susan MacDonald. My name is Safi Thi-Kim Felce and I too survived the crash. I am 27 years old now and still it bothers me. My feelings are mixed and even though I am older now, I don't think the pain and emotional scars will ever go away. I suffered a fractured skull, two broken legs and brain damage.

"I actually went back to Vietnam nearly five years ago. I was filmed out there for a documentary on Vietnamese War Orphans. It was very emotional for me but it was something I have always wanted to do. One of the main reasons was to pay my respects to the others that died. In a way I was "laying the ghost" yet it still haunts me.

"Up until now, I had only kept in touch with a few from the crash, but since Sister Susan got in touch with me again, I have had quite a few e-mails from other adoptees and crash survivors. I am happy that we can keep in touch and possibly meet one day. The thing is, I live in England and kind of feel alone out here. It seems that everyone went to America or Australia!! I know a few went to England but I don't know where."

That was our first correspondence. Safi impressed me with her heart-felt email. I was truly affected by her. It was what I had been in search of -- Babylift kids who wanted to reach out and learn about their beginnings, about the crash or even about the C-5A Galaxy missions. For the first time I felt good about the Babylift mission. I felt the love and appreciation from Safi. She thanked me and all my crew members for her freedom in a world she otherwise would not have known.

When I read about the injuries she sustained it just broke me up inside. She was so small then, less than a year old. I can only imagine how she must have been bounced or thrown around strapped in her seat. She could have been trapped between kids as the aircraft tumbled and slid through the muddy rice paddies. She could have been seated at the end of the row and been thrown against the side wall, causing her head injury. The babies were positioned two babies per seat with 12 seats across in each of the seven rows.

Approximately 150 babies were seated upstairs. Remarkably, we lost only two infants upstairs. One of those died from trauma at impact and the other was strangled by a bag of gold around her neck, according the pilot.

Safi emailed me a second letter to share more about herself. Her letter read:

"I hope you have found comfort in me and any others that may have contacted you. Keeping in contact with someone from the crash has really helped me. I am glad of others that I can talk with and share similar feelings. I will tell you a little about myself.

"I live in Northampton, England, where I was brought after the crash. I have a brother who is Vietnamese, too. My parents adopted him first before they got me. I got a lot of media attention when I arrived and was in the local papers and television. I think it was because my brother and I were the only Vietnamese adoptees in

Northampton. I suppose for a while I grew up confused and wondering if I was English or Vietnamese.

"Anyway I have always been interested in my roots and origins, so much so that I married a Vietnamese here. (He came over by boat with his family later.) My marriage didn't work out because of the cultural differences, but from it I have two children.

"As I said, I was glad of my return trip to Vietnam. It was very emotional for me but it was something I had to do. I was filmed for a documentary. You might have heard or seen it. It was called 'Children of the Ashes.' I'm sure it was shown where you live.

"I'm glad that we can be in touch. So what do you do for a living? If you don't mind me asking, how old are you? Were you by any chance on a news documentary regarding the crash? I'm sure I have heard your name before."

It was signed, "Your new-found friend, Safi"

Safi was absolutely right; she was my new-found friend. We have maintained our friendship to this day. We finally got to meet in person during the 35th anniversary of the C-5A Galaxy crash in Vietnam. Not only did I meet Safi, I met four other survivors of the crash during our reunion. We had a memorial service at the crash site. The adoptees read the names of the kids who died and I read the names of my crew members who died. Sister Susan, others and I also read the names of the women from the DAO (Defense Attaché Office).

I let Safi know that it was possible that she saw me on ABC News 20/20 Magazine in 1984. That show aired nine years to the date of the crash,(April 4, 1984). Safi has a lovely family – two sons and a daughter -- and she'd told them all about me. I felt so gratified to hear them say to me, "Thanks for saving our mom."

Safi and her family sat at the same table with me during the reunion dinner. We got acquainted and shed tears together as we talked about the Babylift. It was difficult for Safi to hear my story; she really got goose bumps as I talked about what went on downstairs.

It was just as difficult for me to tell my story, for several reasons. First, the table was full of folks listening to my every word, and I tried to keep from crying but couldn't hold back my tears. Second, it was tough talking about my injuries because I found myself reliving the pain I suffered and becoming more choked up.

Safi and I embraced each other at the crash site during the memorial service and survivors Joakim, Annabelle, and Emma joined us. We stood there at the crash site holding each other crying and feeling BLESSED ABOUT HAVING A SECOND CHANCE AT LIFE. IT WAS POWERFUL!

**EMMA MCCRUDDEN, PHIL WISE, ANNABELLE
BOMMELAERE, SAFI-THI-KIM DUB, JOAKIM KIM
KRONQVIST, AND BENOIT THOREL**

SAFI-THI-KIM DUB BABY PICTURE.

PHIL WISE, SAFI, WITH EMMA
MCCRUDDEN, ANNABELLE BOMMELAERE,
SURVIVORS OF C5-A GALAXY CRASH, 2010 REUNION
HO-CHI-MHIN CITY, VIETNAM

JOURNAL ENTRY

APRIL 4, 1975 (CONTINUED)

- *I can feel the aircraft cooling off as the engines are at full throttle and the anxiety of each passenger dissipates. Our itinerary is to go to Clark to refuel and on to Travis where President Ford will meet the orphans and welcome them to America. We begin taxing down the runway and the big C5-A Galaxy is rumbling as it picks up speed. I'm sitting on the cargo floor with a cargo tie-down strap across my lap feeling the vibration of the rumbling aircraft. It is excessively noisy as we lift up with the sounds of the wheels closing as they fold into the belly of the aircraft.*

- *Finally we are airborne and climbing. The lighting inside the cargo section is dim. I look and observe the patients and passengers sighing in relief as we climb higher. Sitting on the cold cargo floor I begin to wiggle around trying to find comfort even though a blanket underneath cushions me. About 15 minutes into the flight the seat belt sign is turned off. Lt Aune, DC Johnson and I are up attending to a female patient in distress. We try to calm her down, and Lt. Aune decides to go up to the galley to retrieve some medication for our patient. DC and I stay with the patient.*

SMSgt. Joe Castro is filming us; SSgt. Kenneth Nance is behind me making his way forward of the aircraft; and Col. Willis is walking toward us close to the left side cat walk offering to help with the patient.

- *Suddenly a loud explosion jars the cargo section. I look up toward the aft (rear) of the cargo where the noise comes from and see the rear cargo doors and ramp have torn off like ripped paper. We go into a rapid decompression while I stand there stunned. I look back and see Perkins on the ladder near the top hanging on as he is trying to make it to the troop compartment. At the same time I see the blue skies and the white clouds. And the dim cargo section suddenly illuminates then fills with fog and cold air.*

- *It is cold in the cargo hold section and I hear the fearful voices of the kids yelling and screaming. I see bodies sucked out the rear and pallets of supplies and equipment ripped out, disappearing into the openness. I see the blue skies and white clouds glaring in front of me but death never crosses my mind. Instead, the voice of one of my flight school instructors echoes in my thoughts: SMSgt. Jim Harden said, "Phil if you get into a situation and the airplane is going down make sure you save yourself first." But I am having great difficulty holding on to that thought as I stare at the sky in disbelief trying to breathe but having great difficulty. And all I can think of is how will I protect the babies. I am thrown off my feet as I try to grab hold of a cargo tie-down strap. From that point forward I don't remember what happened. I don't remember the crash landing or any of the rescue efforts. I do have vague memories of hearing helicopter propellers and feeling chilly.*

CHAPTER TWENTY ONE

Official Air Force Investigation

- Rapid decompression; there were several malfunctions of the quick don oxygen masks and fire masks.

SABATAGE/GROUND FIRE ANALYSIS

- The possibility that an internal explosion or an externally fired projectile triggered the failure in the aft ramp was thoroughly explored. All witness statements and indications of possible explosive damage were given detailed analysis.

- Crew interviews and statements reveal that a security watch was established on the ground at Tan Son Nhut. Crewmembers had inspected potential hiding places for explosives devices prior to their departure and found nothing. Prior to the rapid decompression, crew members unanimously stated that they neither heard nor saw anything that could be associated with an explosive. Most of the crewmembers associated all their sensations as very similar to the sound and feel of rapid decompression in the altitude chamber.

- Rumors that the aircraft was taking ground fire during departure could not be confirmed. The investigation team was unable to find anyone who actually saw the reported ground fire. It was concluded that the likelihood of seeing even tracers under daylight conditions would be remote. There was no sound of any hits noted by the crew. In addition, the aircraft had departed small arms environment when the rapid decompression occurred.

- The DAO reported that a 9-year old girl survivor from the cargo compartment saw a red handbag explode. This report was investigated, and the explosion determined to have been caused by the rapid decompression due to trapped air in handbag. Interviews with crewmembers that had assessed the damage revealed that there was an open red handbag and it was open after the decompression. If it had contained an explosive device, the bag would have been destroyed. Additionally, any explosion from the baggage would have caused noticeable damage to the interior of the aircraft. No related damage was noted by the crew or during the investigation.

- On three separate occasions, EOD (explosive ordinance disposal) personnel searched the crash site for evidence of explosives. An EOD team from the 635 MMS, Utapoa AFB Thailand, arrived at the crash site at 0200H 5 April 1975. Their search failed to uncover any damage that was caused by an explosion. An additional EOD team from the 3rd MMS, Clark AB, P.I. arrived at Tan Son Nhut Air Base at 1300H, 5 April 1975, were briefed by the 635 MMS team, and proceeded to crash site. Their search of the crash site was also negative. However, they did recover a hand grenade from near the vertical stabilizer. The grenade had not completely detonated and was most probably equipment carried by an ARVN soldier who had been struck by the aircraft during the crash landing. When the accident investigation personnel arrived at the crash site, a third search of the wreckage was made. An explosive detector dog and the 3rd MMS EOD Team checked all aircraft components, which the investigation team members could identify as areas susceptible to explosive damage. Results of the detector dog crash site activities were negative. The detector dog was then used to check aircraft components as they were recovered and placed in a hanger at Clark AB. As a final check for explosives, a detector dog checked components from the aircraft when they arrived at San Antonio ALC. During this check, the dog-alerted on three separate components. However, they were sent to the FBI laboratory for chemical analysis and the FBI lab tests were negative.

History of Flight:

- The C-5A SN 68-218 departed Travis Air Base on 1 April 1975, it onloaded cargo at Warner Robins AFB, GA. with in route stops before landing at Clark Air Base Philippines for crew rest. On April 4, the mission departed Clark for Tan Son Nhut Air Base South Vietnam.

- Upon arrival at Tan Son Nhut Air Base the offloading was completed. (Note: This was the first occasion for the aft (rear) doors to be opened since the onload at Warner Robins.) Preparation was made for the onload of passengers. After the onload of passengers the engines were started and takeoff was made at 0803Z (1603 L, or 4:03 pm).

- After takeoff, a right hand turn was initiated and the aircraft proceeded direct to Vung Tau. The aircraft passed Vung Tau at0812Z (1603 L), climbing through FL200 (flight level 20,000 ft). At 0815 Z a rapid decompression occurred as the aircraft was climbing through 23,372 feet, air speed 254 knots, and a heading of 136 degrees. The crew donned oxygen masks and established interphone contact. Immediately following the decompression, the number one and number two hydraulic systems were lost (including pressure and quantity). Approximately 45 seconds after the decompression, a shallow descending left was begun for an emergency return to Saigon.

• As the damage was being assessed, the pilot realized that he had no pitch control. He asked the copilot to assist him with the pitch; however, the copilot's pitch control was also inoperative. During the descent the airspeed increased to 300 knots, the nose of the aircraft began to rise, and the airspeed began to rapidly decrease. To prevent the aircraft from entering the stall speed range, a right bank of 30-40 degrees was made and power reduced. The aircraft then entered a steep dive. The wings were leveled, and the pilot observed a rapid increase in airspeed. Realizing that his only means of pitch control was power and bank, he added power to arrest the dive. As the airspeed increased through 326 knots, the nose of the aircraft began to rise. From this point on the pilots developed techniques for some limited control of pitch through cautious use of power and bank and established a controllable rate of descent at 250-260 knots.

• The initial assessment of damage revealed that the pressure door, a large portion of the ramp, and center cargo door had departed the aircraft. Initially both side cargo doors were observed to be attached to the aircraft but subsequent observations revealed the right hand side cargo door was missing. A large portion of the torque deck was missing and numerous cables were hanging from the sloping torque deck area immediately aft (rear) of the pressure bulkhead.

• An emergency was declared and the aircrew was briefed to prepare for an emergency landing at Tan Son Nhut. The undivided attention of the pilots was directed to aircraft control. While the pilot maintained power requirements, the copilot flew the ailerons.

• Seeing that they would be unable to reach the runway, the pilots rolled the wings level and applied power to the full throttle capability (full throttle quadrant). All landing gear were noted in the down and lock position by the flight engineer. Immediately prior to impact, the pilot restarted the throttles to idle. The aircraft touched down at 1630H (4:30 pm) in a rice paddy/marsh area approximately 2 NM (nautical miles) NE of the runway. The aircraft was in a slightly left wing low, level flight attitude with an airspeed above 269 knots. It rolled and slid along the ground for 1000 feet and became airborne, attaining a flight path angle of approximately 12 degrees. The aircraft continued in flight for 2700 feet during which time the Saigon River was crossed. The second impact was on the western bank of the river at which time the aircraft skidded and broke into four major sections (tail, flight deck, troop, and wing). The cargo compartment disintegrated as the aircraft progressed down the touchdown path.

• After coming to a stop, the surviving crew members and medical team evacuated the passengers in the troop compartment and surrounding area to the best of their ability. Rescue helicopters arrived approximately 5 minutes after cash.

Findings:

- While climbing through FL 233, a material failure of either the #3 tie rod assembly, the #3 bell crank arm or the #4 bell crank arm (most probably the #3 tie rod) in combination with an existing out of rig condition allowed the #1, 2, and 3 locks on the right side of the ramp to unlock.

- The unlocking of the right side locks 1, 2, and 3 created an instantaneous overload on the aft (rear) ramp structure and the #4 thru #7 locks causing the ramp structure to fall resulting in a decompression.

- The right side of the ramp moved down, tearing the ramp right to left along ramp station 33, rotated approximately 90 degrees around the left side ramp locks and then separated from the aircraft.

- As the ramp dropped and started its right-to-left rotation, the pressure door, still attached to the ramp, tilted to the right until the pressure door fingers moved off the upper fuselage fixed beam reaction point rollers. The pressure door split vertically from top to bottom at LBL 28, struck the sloping torque deck and, in conjunction with pressurization air, caused the number 1 and number 2 hydraulic lines, stabilizer trim, rudder and elevator cables to be severed. In addition, some electrical wiring on the left side of the hayloft/fuselage wall was severed.

**PHIL AT CRASH SITE HOLDING INSULATION FROM
C5A GALAXY WRECKAGE, APRIL 4, 2010**

CHAPTER TWENTY TWO
From the Journal of Dan Halen

"On the day after the C-5 crash, I was assigned as an Aero Medical Evacuation Technician (AET) to crew a C-141 Aero Medical Evacuation mission to Tan San Nhut AB, RVN, along with two other AETs (SMSgt. Tim Falls, SSgt. Wayne Everingham, and two nurses from the 9th* AES. This was important since this meant that we had a mixed crew and the technicians were all qualified on the C-141, C-9, and C-130 aircraft; nurses were not qualified on the C-141 aircraft. Since they had only been qualified to crew the C-9, the nurses were in a foreign environment and were very frightened. The mission as outlined to us was to pick up approximately 180 Vietnamese orphans who were being brought to the base from the local orphanages near the base to be flown to safety since the base and the area around it were about to fall, or had already fallen into the hands of the Viet Cong (VC).*

When we landed we had onboard the aircraft a helicopter, two half-tracks and other such equipment to be given to the VNs at the base. I could not understand that since the city was already being overrun by VC, and we could hear the fighting from our position as soon as we opened the aircraft and there was no ground crew to meet us. However, ours was not to reason why.

One of our major concerns, other than the safety of the aircraft and crew, was our ability to maintain the capability to restart the aircraft if we shut it down in the absence of a ground power unit and crew to run it. So it was decided that we would do a "Hot Load," which meant keeping the onboard auxiliary power unit (APU) running to provided aircraft power while on the ground and restart engines when needed. This would limit our time because of the fuel consumption.

We were told that we would only be on the ground about one hour, but that soon ran to well over two hours because, as it was explained to us, the orphans were being delayed at various check points between Saigon and the base. We were extremely concerned since the base already had VCs on it and we could hear the sound of firing getting nearer to the flight line.

After about 2.5 hours a bus arrived with 44 people aboard, none of which were Vietnamese orphans. There were, as I remember, 38 American men, two women (wives of two of the men), and four dependent children of these Americans. The men were all identified to us as employees of World Airways, Flying Tigers, or other US contract airlines who had been left after the base was evacuated, and had no other way out of the country.

We felt duped since we had willingly accepted the risks of the mission thinking that we were being sent to rescue "orphans."Another major concern for us was that we had heard various stories about what might have caused the C-5 crash, including that there had been some "white milky substance" found that could have caused an explosion. The other technicians and I decided that for our safety we would have to limit what was brought aboard the aircraft.

We made the passengers empty their luggage and other belongings out on the ground, and we went through each item and also searched each individual. What we found was startling. We found drugs (heroin, cocaine, and marijuana), along with precious stones and metals (gold and silver), which were hidden in the bags or taped around the bodies of the women. We later found that the religious shrines had been looted for the stones and metals since the currency had no value after the fall of the country. Yours,

DAN HALEN, Retired USAF

**PATIENTS, VOLUNTEERS AND PASSENGERS IN CARGO
HOLE SECTION BEFORE TAKE-OFF APRIL 4, 1975. THIS
IS THE SECTION OF THE PLANE PHIL WISE WAS IN AT
TAKEOFF
(COURTESY OF LARRY ENGLEMANN/TONY COALSON)**

- *The sounds of helicopters hovering echo in my ears but I am unconscious. I vaguely remember the sounds but I am placed in a triage situation awaiting evacuation to the Seventh Day Adventist hospital in Saigon, and I am unaware . Later, crew members who picked me up from the hospital tell me that I raised hell while I was being treated. They say I needed emergency surgery to stop the bleeding from my head, leg and arm wounds but that I would not let any of the Vietnamese medical team treat me. I don't know why but maybe my subconscious took over and protected me from what I thought was the enemy.*

- *They tell me I fought off nurses and doctors who were trying to treat me. I don't settle down until a European nurse treats me. In my state, I must think she is an American nurse, and I allow her to sedate me and take me to surgery. I know none of this consciously.*

- *Back at the base the word gets out that the C5-A has crashed with a plane load of babies. My good friends Jim Harden and Denise Johnke are at the squadron on alert duty when they get word that there are no survivors. My friends reject those thoughts right away by saying "Not*

Phil, if anybody survives, it's Phil." They refuse to believe that I am dead.

- *Denise is right there with me when I arrive back at Clark. She remains by my side from the flight line up until I go through the surgical doors, dazed in that metal light green hospital bed. I am in and out of consciousness , unaware of the memorable details Denise is witnessing.*

CHAPTER TWENTY THREE

Many kids passed through my hands as we lifted each one up the stairs and placed them in their seats on the C5-A Galaxy. It's hard to say which of those kids I've now met as adults. However briefly I held them, it is rewarding for me to know that I have met a few all these years later.

The first time I met adoptees was in St. Louis at Sister Susan MacDonald's invitation, in July 2001. One young man who stood out was Daniel Tran Bischoff, who really wanted to meet me. Dan was one of those who passed through my hands on April 4, 1975. Dan had been adopted by Dick and Ann Bishcoff, university professors who raised him in University City, Missouri.

Sister Susan reserved a suite at the Holiday Inn in St. Louis, and I was the guest speaker for that long-awaited Babylift reunion. It had been 26 years since I was last in contact with any of the kids of Operation Babylift in person. Eight adoptees attended this reunion: Daniel Tran Bischoff, Christy Beachler, Ryan Killacky, Noelle Rocklage, Warren Dalal, Dana Pena, Evelyn Peters, and Casey Borgman. I was honored to be a part of Sister Susan's reunion program on her first time hosting such an event.

I'll never forget meeting Dan. He and the others were in the conference room when I arrived; and as soon as I walked in, my man Dan rushed over to me and said, "Phil, what an honor to meet you!"

We hugged and embraced each other, and I choked up right away. I could not believe how dynamic this young man was. He thanked me, my crew members, and expressed his condolences for the loss of life to my fallen crew members. When Dan mentioned the crew members, I just melted inside. For years I wondered if any of the Babylift kids would recognize the sacrifices of my fallen crew members. Daniel Tran Bischoff was the first to do so. Each time I visit the Vietnam Veteran Memorial Wall, I tell my fallen crew members that Daniel Bischoff and other C-5A Galaxy Operation Babylift survivors are truly grateful for their sacrifices.

Each time Sister Susan introduced me to another adoptee, we hugged one another and I learned a little about each of them. The highlight of the reunion was when I sat down with them and shared my personal story. They asked many questions and were intently focused on my every word. Dan wanted to know how he was positioned in the aircraft, how many kids per seat, who worked in the troop compartment, if there were paper work accompanying him or whether or not he was wearing a wrist band.

And he asked about my injuries and all about my family and my life. He showed genuine concern and interest in me. What impressed me about Dan was he wanted to put the pieces together about his origin and the Babylift mission. He also wanted to thank everyone involved in his rescue.

Many of us traveled from different parts of the country and it was the first time some of the adoptees met each other. We had dinner at the hotel restaurant and had a great time sharing stories. Sister Susan was extremely happy and very joyful for all of us. Dan found out from Sister Susan that he was moved from Pere Olivier Orphanage in Saigon on April 2, 1975. After surviving the C-5A Galaxy crash, he was placed on a Pam Am flight on April 5, 1975.

The day after I spoke at the reunion, Dan invited me to dinner to meet his parents, who were very warm and gracious toward me. They, too, thanked me and my crew members for the gift of Daniel. They shared with me how Dan wanted to know all about the Babylift from a very early age. He knew that he looked different from other kids in his neighborhood and was set on researching Operation Babylift. His parents talked about how Dan went to the Lockheed Aircraft Corporation and researched the C-5A Galaxy.

Lockheed learned about Dan being a survivor aboard the C-5A and gave him a tour of its Georgia Corporate Office. They gave him a model aircraft of the C-5A Galaxy; Dan treasures it and keeps it on the fireplace mantel at his parent's house. I loved it and we took pictures of Dan and me holding it.

Dan has written about his return trip to Vietnam. It was something he had to do. He talks about meeting young orphans at Phu My orphanage in Gia Dinh, a suburb of Saigon. Remarkably, Dan visited the orphanage alone and found himself surrounded by kids. One, who was lying on a tiled floor, grabbed Dan's hand and held onto it tightly, all the while looking up at him smiling. At that point Dan felt himself crying. Dan was picturing that kid as himself 25 years earlier.

Dan went to the crash site the next day to pay his respects at a memorial service. Participants released 76 balloons bearing the names of the kids who were known to have died there. Releasing the balloons "felt good," Dan wrote. I believed it represented not only a tribute to the fallen ones but a letting go of all the uncertainty of the past. When telling his story, Dan pays tribute to Sister Mary Nelle Gage, Sister Marie Marte, and Rose Mary Taylor -- all who worked and supervised the orphanages. Dan credits his privileged life to these women and his adopted family. In July of 2001 Dan wrote an e-mail to me, Bud, and Regina. It reads:

"Many different thoughts and emotions regarding the Galaxy crash have been circulating around my brain lately. It's a lot to chew on... and I try not to think about it on a daily basis, but sometimes I just can't help it. However, I do feel that I am being more honest about everything with myself. I'm listening, reading, watching, and learning everything I can about everything... not just the crash but all the 100s of people that are somehow intertwined with the event. The people that were actually aboard the aircraft are (and always will) have a special place in my being.

"The recent opportunity to meet Sgt. Phil Wise was amazing. Phil is the first C-5 survivor I've met who was an adult at the time of the crash. So his perspective and memories of the day are unlike any accounts I have heard. I was just a baby. I don't remember a damn thing! It was quite a gift to meet Phil, and I'm very much looking

forward to meeting you Regina, and Bud. Yes... it will be quite a day. Phil's stories gave such a unique view for me of that day, that I eagerly await any future meetings with all of you.

"*I have not, upon becoming very busy with other aspects of my little life, given much attention or added research to my book idea regarding the crash. In fact, there are days when I question whether or not I should write one at all? I realize now that there is no hurry, as I earlier thought... I think time and age will only make my perceptions of that day and my life clearer. It would be immature of me to think I could accurately write about something that happened to me as an infant. I need both time and the 'hits' of life to better appreciate what I was earlier considering.*"

Dan believes there is tremendous strength to be gained from meeting and getting to know all who were aboard the C-5A Galaxy on that Saigon day. Each time I go to St. Louis I always call my friend Dan and say hello.

On one of my birthdays, to my surprise Dan sent me a model C-5A Galaxy aircraft. It was identical to the one he had on his parents' mantel. I was overwhelmed by his generosity and thoughtfulness. I often tell the story about Dan when I'm speaking and always take along with me the C-5A Galaxy model.

Dan recently mailed me a medal that reads "VIETNAM VETERANS NATIONAL MEDAL." Inscribed on the Medal: "VIETNAM VETERANS MEMORIAL: In honor of the courage, sacrifice and devotion to duty of the men and women who served their country during the Vietnam War."

The medal is in a special place in my living room showcase. Daniel Tran Bischoff is a special person in my life. I wish him much happiness and I hope he finds all the answers he's looking for.

**THE
BISCHOFF
FAMILY**

PHIL WISE AND DANIEL BISCHOFF

CHAPTER TWENTY FOUR

The day I arrived in St Louis for Sister Susan's first reunion in July 2001, Ryan Killacky was there to pick me up, sent by Sister Susan. He and I got acquainted as we rode to my hotel. Ryan was not on the C-5A Galaxy; rather he had been transported on a Pam Am flight and was adopted into a loving family from Illinois.

All the adoptees Sister Susan introduced me to were very impressive young people. It was my honor to speak to these wonderful Americans who simply wanted to hear a crew member's account of what happened with Operation Babylift.

Ryan is another Babylift alum I've kept in touch with over the years. When I received an invitation to attend an award ceremony in Virginia Beach, Virginia, I shared the information with him. The award ceremony was hosted by Freddy Moody of Minorities in the Military; and I was being recognized for my involvement with Operation Babylift. Sister Susan MacDonald, Byron Noone, Lana Noone, Shirley Peck Barnes and Tia Keevil also were honored for their role in Operation Babylift.

The Virginian Pilot Newspaper covered the story and wrote an article about it the following day. I sent the article to Ryan and he loved it. He replied by saying:

"Thank you for forwarding the article. I have to admit that I cried when I read it. As a 28-yea-old male, I can only now feel comfortable crying and not feel ashamed or like a 'sissy'. Though I was not old enough to remember the events during the time I was born into, I feel much compassion and gratitude for people like you, who gave me the opportunity to live. I can never say or express my sincere gratitude enough, nor give back all that was given to me.
"Know that the actions you took during your tour and number of children you saved go well above the call of duty.

"I am a member of the Illinois Dept. of Corrections Honor Guard; like the Military Honor Guard we honor those killed in the

line of duty. I carry myself very respectfully when posting the Colors and representing fellow fallen officers. I can never truly experience what you have gone through but know the importance of our freedom and not forgetting those who sacrificed their lives for what they believe in.

"I am grateful to have met you and look forward to continuing our friendship. Hope you and your family are doing well."
Respectfully,
Ryan Killacky.

Ryan is a very classy young man. Once again here's an example of a Babylift adoptee who appreciates the freedom of this country and loves America. Working in law enforcement is Ryan's way of giving back to a grateful nation. I am proud of Ryan and extremely honored to have him as a friend.

PHIL WISE AND RYAN KILACKY

JOURNAL ENTRY
APRIL 6, 1975

- *I wake up in ICU at Clark Air Base Republic of the Philippines, and I feel a pressure in my abdomen. I try to reach my groin area but restraints are on my wrists. At this point I don't know that there is a Foley catheter placed in me. I look over to my left side and I see Greg Gmerek lying in the bed next to me. I say to Greg, "Hey man you are not as banged up as I am." He shouts out: "Phil, you are alive, thank you, thank you." I say, "For what?" He answers, "You saved my life by assigning me to work in the troop compartment. I might not have been as lucky as you in the cargo hold section."*

- *I realize that I have survived the airplane crash. My head is bandaged, my left eye is bandaged, and my left leg is elevated and extended in the air with a cast on it. Both arms are bandaged. My chest is bandaged, too. I have multiple lacerations all over my body. When Greg shouts my name the entire nursing staff in the room rushes over to me to check me out. One says, "We were waiting on you to wake up so we can rush you back to surgery." I do not know that I have been through surgery twice before. They* have to drain the infection out of my left leg. My mangled left leg is severely infected due to opened wounds that were exposed to the muddy rice paddy where we touched down. I go through surgery again and I am moved from ICU to a ward. I am then placed in quarantine for two weeks and unable to receive visitors. While in quarantine I receive intramuscular injections of antibiotics four times a day. The Vietnamese farmers fertilize their rice paddies with cow manure and other bacteria-infested material. That's why I have to go through intense antibiotic therapy. This treatment goes on for a period of six weeks. My arm and buttocks are like raw meat from taking so many shots.

- My first visitor is Colonel Waxtein from the Pentagon, and he debriefs me. He wants to know my account of what happened on the C5-A crash. Colonel Waxtein tells me I am the only survivor that made it out of the cargo hold section and how blessed I am. He thanks me for my service and departs with his report and tape recorder heading back to Washington D.C.

CHAPTER TWENTY FIVE

We began our family reunion on Friday, July 1, 2011 with a meet and greet day. My wife, my daughter and son, along with his daughter and wife, were there meeting and greeting. It was the first time my son and his wife and daughter were meeting many of my family. This was only the second family reunion we had ever had. Meet and greet day was fun for people getting acquainted with family members they hadn't seen in years. I was in charge of cooking the meat, therefore I couldn't socialize much. My day was to start at 5 a.m., and I was up and ready to get going. But my brother-in-law was late to pick me up. I wanted to have the cook fire burning by 6 a.m. and bro-in-law showed at 6:15a.m.

Time was important because we had to cook 22 slabs of ribs, 80 lbs of chicken, and had to grill hot dogs and hamburgers. I managed to get the fire going about 6:30 a.m., and shortly afterwards I put the meat on. The three grillers -- cousin Darius, CB (bro-in-law) and I – had a busy morning. Family members started arriving around 9:30 - 10:00 a.m. One by one, they made their way over to the grilling area. The weather was beginning to heat up and the meat was cooking and smelling good.

Many family members wanted to hold conversations, but we had to keep our eyes on the meat. I missed out on getting acquainted with everybody early on but was able to fellowship later. My parents were extremely happy to be there. My father and his living siblings, two sisters and a brother, had a great time. I was struck by how different they looked in their later years from the way they had when I was growing up.

When they were younger, they partied and laughed and joked a lot when they got together. This time was noticeably different. They only smiled and grinned as they stared at each other. I know my dad is suffering from an early form of dementia. My Aunt Doll is the youngest sibling and she is cool, very sharp and energetic. She has aged beautifully and gracefully. Aunt Edna, the oldest of all the siblings, looks grand and strong. She gets around very well and has a great conversation for you. Uncle Otis was more laid back and passive. He was in great shape physically but I could tell his diabetes affected his overall health. My dad mostly listened to everybody's conversations. He looked good for 86 years old.

After graduating from high school, I had lived with Aunt Doll while looking for a job in Detroit at one of the GM, Ford, or Chrysler plants before I decided to join the Air Force. Aunt Doll was a very positive influence in my life; she listened to me and advised me whenever she thought I needed it. All she requested of me was to do my chores, look for a job and stay out of trouble.

I was a home-bound person, a loner, and I didn't like hanging out with others in Detroit. I remember one time I was driving Aunt Doll's 1967 Electra 225 and had an accident on the freeway. I was afraid of what she might say.

When I took her wrecked car home, I told her what happened and how I damaged her car. It was winter time and I had hit an ice patch on the freeway. She was so calm and understanding. She simply said, "Honey, I'm just glad that you are alright." I was so relieved. I didn't want her to be mad at me, because she was my friend. We could talk about anything. We always laughed and listened to good jazz music together.

Uncle Otis was, and still is, my man. He taught me much about the game of pocket billiards. I would watch him play pool and finesse his way around the pool table, and one day I thought I would be able to do that, too. Uncle Otis would play marbles with my brothers and me. He really looked out for me and had my best interest at heart. When I lived in Detroit with Aunt Doll, Uncle Otis made sure I had extra cash in my pocket. He was proud that I was always looking for work. When he came by Aunt Doll's after work he would let me drive his car to run errands for him and my auntie.

Uncle Otis just knew that I would be alright. He would often say, "You won't be like those other boys." He knew I would make something of myself.

Aunt Edna is the oldest child of Roosevelt Wise Sr. and Magdalene Givens Wise. She had nine kids and most of them grew up with my siblings and me. Her oldest, Erwin, was raised down south. Aunt Edna was so sweet and adoring toward me. She would never say no to me wanting to spend the night at her house, and she was more liberal than my mom. We could do things at her house that Mom would not tolerate. She allowed us to stay out later, and let us ride our bikes in the streets or watch the adults play a hand of Bid Whist.

One day my brother Kerwin got in trouble because he and his best friend, Donald Ray, had stolen candy from Johnnie Caldwell's store. Mr. Caldwell told my father and Donald Ray's father what they had done.

Dad and Mister Gene, Donald's dad, always played their numbers at Johnnie Caldwell's store and shot the breeze with each other while having a quart-sized bottle of Strotz beer. Dad came back from the store feeling a little good and Kerwin had no idea that Dad knew about the theft. Mr. Gene got home about the same time as my dad. We were close neighbors and we could hear Donald Ray getting his butt whooped. Kerwin heard his buddy yelling and screaming and he knew why.

Kerwin immediately started crying because he knew Dad had just left Caldwell's store. I didn't know why Kerwin was crying and why Donald Ray was getting a whooping. Dad called Kerwin to come into his bedroom and Kerwin was too afraid to go; in fact he refused to go. Kerwin was so frightened he ran outside and took off running down the alleyway. Dad came out of his bedroom looking for Kerwin and saw him running.

Dad said, "Phillip go after that boy."

When I caught up to Kerwin, he tearfully begged and bargained with me not to take him back home and even offered me money. He pulled 10 cents out of his pocket…five pennies and a nickel to pay me. I couldn't help but laugh and picked Kerwin up and threw him over my shoulders and carried him home. Once at home Kerwin started bargaining with Dad, offering him money and pleading with him not to whoop him. Dad started laughing so hard he couldn't whoop him; in fact all of us were laughing. Those really were the good old days.

Our last family reunion was in 2004. It was very different compared to this year's reunion because at the first, not many family members showed up or registered. We learned a lot from experience, and the 2011 reunion brought family together like we were a long time ago.

PHIL, HIS MOTHER AND BROTHERS AND SISTERS, 1978

CHAPTER TWENTY SIX

Memorial Day meant that school would be out soon. That was a time when we looked forward to the barbeques and riding to Potter's Lake for the fireworks show. It was a fun time for us kids, not knowing the real meaning of Memorial Day.

When I got older I learned the meaning. Many soldiers were coming home in caskets from Vietnam and they were always honored on Memorial Day. The President of the USA would lay a wreath at the tomb of the Unknown Soldier; it was significant to me because there were so many soldiers missing in action in Vietnam. Every Memorial Day holiday the list of MIA soldiers would grow. They were young Americans fighting an unpopular war.

After the war I thought the number of dead soldiers who died in the Vietnam war was ridiculous and the Memorial Day holiday was beginning to sadden me. Each Memorial Day still saddens me. I think about my lost crew members who died on the C-5A Galaxy crash and how I could have died with them on April 4, 1975.

The Memorial Day holiday now makes me realize how blessed I am to have these additional 36 years of living in our beautiful country. I appreciate the sacrifices of all who gave their lives in defense of America.

I had the honor to speak at the 15th anniversary of the Women's Vietnam Veterans Memorial Wall in Washington, DC. I shared the story of Captain Mary Therese Klinker. Capt. Klinker was a flight nurse who selflessly gave her life on board the C-5A Galaxy crash while performing her duties during Operation Baby Lift. The celebration took place on Veteran's Day November 2007.

Prior to the doors blowing off most of our medical crew were attending to patients and comforting the kids. Captain Klinker was in the aft (rear) area along with Michael Paget when the doors blew off. Unfortunately, Michael took a direct hit from the debris flying out through the open doorway and was severely injured. Captain Klinker immediately went to him and began trying to drag him to a safer area and away from the gaping hole in the rear. The cargo section quickly filled with fog.

I was struggling to breathe while hanging onto a cargo tie strap. I told the audience about Captain Klinker's brave actions during a pivotal time of the rapid decompression. Captain Mary Klinker put aside her own safety to rescue a fellow crew member. My position was forward of the aircraft when the doors blew off; therefore I was not in as much danger as Mary Klinker, Michael Paget and Denning C. Johnson.

I believe anyone who was not sucked out of the rear entrance during decompression remained alive until the plane hit the ground. Each Veterans Day I find myself reflecting on that daunting day. The loss of so many soldiers during the Vietnam War leaves me with a sadness about that era. So many of my generation were drafted to fight for our country and some of us volunteered, but many fled to Canada and elsewhere. I felt a sense of duty to defend America although I was scared as hell. When I look back on my decision to enlist into the Air Force I don't regret a thing. I thank God for America; we are the savior of the free world.

Coming home to an unappreciative country where many called us baby killers was hard to swallow. I kept quiet about my involvement in Vietnam, fearing that I would be scorned as well. I wore clothing that covered my wounds just to avoid questions about them. I was not only not ready talk about the crash but was also embarrassed to say I was in Vietnam.

Now, it's cool to be a veteran: America has learned its lesson when it comes to veterans fighting wars and coming home. America is more compassionate and supportive for our fighting men and women. It took the loss of more than 58,000 lives for America to wake up. Veterans Day is our day and I am proud to be a veteran.

CHANGE OF COMMAND CEREMONY, 1975

JOURNAL ENTRY
MAY 1975

- *I am finally released from quarantine and am able to receive visitors. Tessie hasn't seen me since the night before the crash and she is a nervous wreck waiting to learn about my condition. She gets word of the crash through my friend Ted Coleman. He escorts her on base to visit me. When they come to see me I learn that the hospital administrator has placed signs throughout the hospital corridors on the first floor that read: no visitors for Sergeant Wise.*

- *It is nice to know that so many friends care about me and I feel bad that they have been turned away. My good friend Ted (Tico) Coleman gets Tessie a daily base pass authorized by the Base Commander. She is able to visit with me every day; I appreciate her helping to take care of me. Tessie is hands on when comes to my health care needs and pain management. She calls my nurse whenever I am in pain or any type of discomfort. Tessie gets to know my mother by way of telephone. She calls her almost daily, giving her an update on my condition. That's what Tessie is really about, loving, caring, thoughtful, and considerate. Mom loves Tessie right away and can hardly wait to meet her.*

- *Once the word gets out that my quarantine is over I begin to receive visitors. I have so many visitors. My crew members are some of the first to visit, including Marcie and Harriet. They are so excited to see me, they embrace and hug me. And tell me all the details of what went on during the C5-A crash. Lieutenant Goffinet draws a diagram detailing how the C5-A touches down and eventually crash lands in the rice paddies two miles from Saigon.*

- *Marcie and Harriet tell me that I am the only survivor to make it out of the cargo hold section. They don't know at the time that two others survived the cargo hold section, too. Two more crew members come by; at least I think they are crew member because they wear flight suits. What I don't know is that they are CIA. The CIA was at crash site to protect the aircraft wreckage from the local villagers who were pillaging the crash site.*

- *Those guys visit with me and see about my recovery. They thought I was not going to make it when they last saw me in Vietnam. They go on to tell me how they rescued me. Soon, I can't remember their names and I am hoping to meet them again to thank them for saving my life. One of the guys says he saw my white shirt from a distance. They went to check out the burning wreckage and saw me hanging* upside down with my left leg entangled in wire cable. I am told that I was unconscious with my forehead laid open, my eyeball protruding out of its socket and multiple wounds all over my body. While they were untangling my body from the wreckage they said to each other, "Dang, this dude is still alive." Listening to these guys telling me how they rescued me is riveting. I am hanging on their every word. I give them both a big hug and thank them immensely for saving my life. I think I will never see them again.

CHAPTER TWENTY SEVEN

The road to recovery began with many friends and families sending me get well cards from throughout the USA. The church I grew up in, Bethel United Methodist Church, sent cards weekly wishing me a speedy recovery. My mom wrote me tons of letters wishing me well and praying for me. My friends in the barracks sent me get well cards, too. The crash of the C-5A Galaxy was big news at Clark AB Philippines.

The word got out quickly that I was on the airplane that went down in Vietnam. Initially it was reported that everybody had died, and a series of false reports about the crash followed. My close friend Curtis Smith did not believe them. Curtis and I stayed in the same barracks and we often partied together off base. He told our friends, "There's no way Gangster is gone." That's what they called me: Gangster! The name Gangster was my handle as a pool player and it reflected my style of playing pool -- smooth and dangerous.

All of the aerovac technicians stayed at the same barracks. So, Curtis was one of the first to get the news about me surviving the airplane crash. He was so happy to hear that news, he told everybody that I was alive. I wasn't evacuated from Vietnam until a day later, so many of my friends wanted to visit me. When I arrived back at Clark, I was barely hanging onto life. Curtis, a very religious person, started praying for my recovery. He had his mother and her church members pray for me, too.

Curtis and Bird Johnson got together and had all my friends in the barracks sign a card for me. Curtis mom's church members from Stockton California sent me cards regularly. Some of the cards had money in them; some had personal notes written to me. I really believe all their prayers and love propelled me to recovery.

While I was in quarantine the first couple of weeks, every day, many, many people were trying to get in to visit me, only to get turned away. Get well cards just kept coming. I didn't know I had so much love out there.

My co-workers at 9th AEG (Aero Medical Evacuation Group) were especially supportive. They prayed for me and handled my military affairs. When Harriet and Marcie visited, I was so happy to see them; I was in pain but had to hug them. They looked good and showed no signs of injuries from being in the crash. Marcie and Harriet said, "Phil we can't believe you survived the cargo section. Everybody died downstairs. How did you do it?"

They shared with me the details of what happened and who we lost. They drew a diagram of the path the pilot took when the aircraft crash landed. The diagram showed how we bellied down on one side of the Saigon River and went airborne and bellied down on the other side of the river. I was astonished to hear the level of destruction the plane underwent.

The pastor of Curtis's mom's church invited me to come and visit Emmanuel Baptist Church once I got well. I took the pastor up on his offer and visited the church as soon as I got back to the States. Curtis picked me up from Travis Air Force Base, California. He had just brought a brand new Chrysler Cordoba and was excited to show it to me. We drove to his mom's house in Stockton where I met his parents and one of his sisters. It was great to finally meet Mrs. Smith; she was very warm and a very charming lady. She was excited to meet me and wanted know if I was going to church with them Sunday. I said, "Yes ma'am! I've been looking forward to meeting your church members. They helped me so much with their prayers during my recovery."

Mrs. Smith prepared a lovely dinner, we talked and got acquainted. They wanted to know about my injuries and how long would I need my cane. They really showed a lot of love and affection. The next day we went to Emmanuel Baptist Church, the congregation really showed up that day and filled the church completely. The Smith family walked in the church ahead of Curtis and me. We were dressed in suits freshly tailored in the Philippines.

We wore shoes with six-inch heels, and I had my cane with me. We were decked out, my friends. We took our seats and the service got started. Toward the end of the service the pastor recognized me and told the story about my participation in Operation Babylift.

He preached about the power of healing through the hands of God and talked about my injuries. He really got the congregation going as I sat there listening in tears and feeling very moved and emotional. I felt something come over me, and suddenly the preacher asked me to stand. I stood up with my cane beside me. The preacher asked me to walk to the pulpit and I did. Normally walking without my cane was difficult, but for some reason I did not need my cane when I walked down the aisle toward the pulpit. I started walking, my left leg felt good, and I was walking without a limp; then I started strutting and the preacher was urging me on, saying "Keep walking my brother, keep walking, son."

People reached out to touch me while I was walking toward the pulpit and when I walked back to my seat, they were grabbing me just wanting to be touched by me.

After the service, a large crowd gathered around, wanting to ask questions about the crash. Some wanted to know if I was the only survivor. I had to dispel some of what they had heard.

RECOVERING AT CLARK HOSPITAL PHILIPPINES, 1975

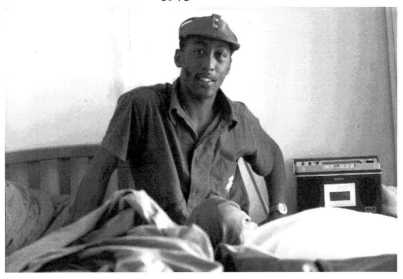

CHAPTER TWENTY EIGHT

"When you believe anything that you don't understand...*then you suffer*". – Steveland Morris, *Superstition*

What do you believe in? What do you believe beyond the ordinary? The status quo? The reality of everyday? Do you believe in things you can't see? That old saying is believe only what you can see! It doesn't really hold up when you think about it, does it? I mean you can't see the air and yet it is there and it is real. You can't see gravity yet it still holds us down whether you believe or not. And what about those intermolecular bonds that hold molecules together so we don't separate and float off into space? Can't see those either, but they're real. And I guess that's what I'm asking, "What is real? What is reality?" If you can't see it, is it not there? But what if you can see it and it is not there. What if it only comes out at night? They only come out at night. The ghosts. Just ask my friend Bernie Duff.

Bernie Duff lives in Vietnam and he's married to Boa Anh, a Vietnamese citizen. Some in the Vietnamese culture believe in ghosts. Bernie, some call him Doc, visited the crash site of the C-5A Galaxy airplane outside Saigon, South Vietnam.

Doc was having a drink in a local tavern and was talking about the crash. Telling people about me. Quietly, no, maybe stealthily, someone joined him.

Doc says, "He was sitting right next to me before I noticed. He stared at me questioningly as to who I was and soon he got comfortable with me and began talking about the crash. His name was Trung. He was a young kid when the C-5A Galaxy crashed in the rice paddies near his home.

"He was flying his kite when he saw the big C-5A Galaxy heading toward him. He dropped his kite and started running away from the incoming aircraft. Trung described the fiery aircraft as it bounced across the rice paddies breaking apart as smoke and fire filled the air. Debris was spread across the rice paddies for over a mile and he told how many villagers went to the crash site and began pillaging the area for aircraft parts and valuables. Dead bodies were fleeced of personal effects such as wallets, jewelry, clothing, and money.

"Trung talked about how his mom made an altar out of an airplane part and placed it outside of her home. Although his mom died shortly after making the Alter, many people come to her home to visit and always visit the altar and say prayers and light incense" He said, "She created the altar to pray for the spirits of all who died on the C-5A Galaxy. She and others that live near the crash site believe the spirits of the dead are still around that sacred ground. In fact, they tell the story about how the ghosts come out at night time."

Trung explained the Chuyen ma ghost stories. He told Doc that the Vietnamese believe in ghosts. To them ghost are the souls of people who died prematurely and usually from a violent and painful end. The ghosts of these dead stay near the site of their death. They believe that the souls live in the afterlife and must be sustained with offerings that include clothes, money food and more. And if it is not offered then the ghosts steal what they need; they are viewed as supernatural robbers, hungry ghosts or ma doi.

Trung told Doc that sometimes the ghost kids will come up and tap people on their shoulders. Trung says that you can see the kids playing near the area where the plane went down. And he says there is always a nurse playing with them and watching over them.

When Doc related this story to me I knew that nurse must be Mary Klinker who was the flight nurse who worked with me in the cargo section. These stories make sense to me because Mary Klinker and all of the DAO volunteers worked with the kids downstairs and were there for them during the rapid decompression. We lost everybody downstairs except for me and two other kids.

**STANDING BESIDE MAKESHIP ALTAR FROM
C5-A GALAXY
WRECKAGE PART OUTSIDE A VILLAGER HOME NEAR
CRASH SITE**

JOURNAL ENTRY
MAY, JUNE, JULY 1975

- *My recovery is long and it seems like every specialist in the hospital has checked me out. One neurosurgeon says that I will have some brain damage or short term memory loss. The orthopedic surgeon thinks my left leg will make a full recovery with intense therapy. Unfortunately I have to go through multiple surgeries to rid the infection in my knee. Initially the eye doctor thinks the vision in my left eye will be affected, but I come through with 20/20 vision.*

- *Physical therapy on my left knee is brutal and will continue for 12 weeks. And each time I come close to gaining full range of motion I go back to surgery for drainage of pus and fluids ,and my leg is placed back in a cast to keep it in place to promote healing. I become quite popular in the hospital rolling through the corridors in my wheel chair as the staff wishes me well.*

- *This month, May 1975, I continue therapy and antibiotic injections to combat the severe, life-threatening infection I incurred from the bacteria in the rice paddies.*

- *A medical technician walks into my room and tosses me the Stars and Stripes newspaper. I see an article about adoptive families suing Lockheed Aircraft Corporation over the loss of their adopted kids. The investigation has determined that faulty locks in the rear cargo doors caused the crash of the C5-A Galaxy.*

- *My recovery continues into June. I have a lot of free time on my hands and I decide to learn how to play chess. Learning is fun and I catch on pretty fast. The guy who teaches me, Jack, is amazed at how fast I learn. Within two weeks I am beating him.. That is good therapy for me. It helps with my emotional state and gives me an outlet to relax and divert the horrific thoughts and memories of the crash.*

- *Outside the hospital at Clark Air Base , the refugees from Vietnam are living in all over the base. They are coming in by the thousands fleeing their homeland for a better future, most arriving by boat but the lucky ones travel by airplane. The Philippines is the first stop in their quest to freedom and many have long journeys to different parts of the world.*

- *The base gymnasium holds some of the children and people who need medical treatment. Volunteers provide food, water, and assistance with documents needed for leaving the country. Many of the refugees cannot speak English. Volunteers have to find military interpreters or English speaking Vietnamese to help.*

- *The influx of refugees continues to flow in well into month of July. And I am still a patient at Clark Air Base Hospital the entire time. I take my first breath of fresh air since the C5-A plane crash in early August. Clark Air Base undergoes a Change of Command ceremony and I leave the hospital to attend. I don't know I am receiving an award until that day. General Paul K. Carlton, the Commander of Military Airlift Command, awards the Airman's Medal to me and three others (Marcie, Greg, and Olen) for our participation in Operation Babylift. We receive the Airman's Medal for heroism. General P.K. Carlton escorts me to my seat after pinning the Airman's Medal on me. My seat is located next to the grandstand. I use my cane to hobble across the parade field. The General takes a liking to me. After the ceremony General Carlton offers me a ride back to the hospital in his limo. His limousine is a long black stretch Ford with four stars across the license plate. I am overwhelmed and a bit star struck but decline his offer. I really appreciate the gesture but want to savor the fresh air and walk because I'd been cooped up in the hospital for more than four months. In its August 1975 edition, the Air Force Times publishes a photo of General Carlton and me.*

CHAPTER TWENTY NINE

I felt a strong pressure in my abdomen. I tried to touch my stomach and suddenly my eyes opened and I saw that my wrists were in restraints. I guess I had been in a deep sleep in the intensive care unit.

The pressure was so discomforting, I gave out a loud moan. Gregg, lying in the bed next to me, pushed his call button and three nurses came running toward me. I complained about the pressure in my stomach. "Take this catheter out so I can pee," I exclaimed. The doctor explained that he was waiting for me to regain consciousness before taking it out. I felt relieved to have it removed.

My hands remained in restraints, my left eye had a patch over it, my vision was blurred, my head was pounding and I was in an awful lot of pain. It seemed like every few minutes the nurses were injecting me with something. The smell of Betadine permeated the room; the trash cans were always full of bandages and gauze.

I was only able to see out of my right eye, so when I looked for Gregg I had to rise up and turn my head. Gregg's bed was to my left and my left eye had a patch over it. Straining to look at him made my head feel like it would explode. The nurses tried to keep me calm by sedating me. I would wake up again and again in excruciating pain.

One time I woke up and found a room full of generals standing by my bedside all smiling at me. As they whispered to each other, I heard one general say, "He survived the C-5 crash and he was the only one that made it out of the bottom."

I began to understand that I was not in a dream and that I really had been in an airplane crash. In my daunting and powerful dreams, I heard things. I felt the cold air and the cold slippery floor. I saw the darkness come to light. The gigantic opening in the rear of the airplane lit up the normally dim cargo section. When I heard the general say that I survived the C-5 crash, I thought, 'Oh my God, I wasn't dreaming."

My heart started racing. I wasn't thinking about my injuries but about my crew members and the kids downstairs with me. And I wondered what the general meant when he said that only I survived. It was hard for me to believe that those kids didn't make it.

What was fuzzy to me then and is still fuzzy to me to this day is who rescued me. After many years of searching for him, I found Bud Traynor, the aircraft commander, who told me that he found me crawling in the muddy rice paddy trying to get back to the wreckage. Although I was unconscious I do recall hearing helicopters hovering. The confusing part to me is what Bud Traynor recalls doesn't add up to what I remember nor what was told to me once I was released from quarantine.

When the two men in flight suits visited my hospital room, I figured they were CIA but I didn't see any name tags. But I remember what they said to me. They said that they were the ones who found me. And that they spotted my white shirt in the burning wreckage and said to each other, "We better save the medic's body so it won't char." According to their version, they rushed over to me and saw my body dangling, hanging upside down. My left leg was entangled in wire cables, my left eye was protruding from its socket, my left leg was bleeding profusely. They said my chest was slashed and bleeding and I didn't look like I was alive.

They began to untangle me and one of them said, "Wow this dude is still alive." And then I was evacuated to the Seventh Day Adventist hospital. Their version of what happened to me is totally different from what Bud Traynor recalled. I remember listening to the two guys and tearing up, feeling grateful that they found me. I sat up in my bed, hugged them both and thanked them for saving my life. I could have been overlooked during the rescue. I've heard stories about how some of the local villagers pillaged the crash site area, taking money and what valuables they could find off the dead.

People even said that some survivors were still alive when the plane crashed but were killed by people who stole their belongings. My friend Gene Siddoway said he went to the morgue and identified the bodies of Captain Mary Klinker, Denning C. Johnson and Michael Paget and brought their bodies back to Clark AB Philippines. Siddoway said our squadron commander (Lt. Col. Noga) ordered that the bodies be retrieved and brought back to Clark Air Base.

Dave Harris said he was on the flight that brought me back to Clark Air Base. He talked about how disoriented I was. He said I smiled a lot and stared, not recognizing the crew I'd worked with many times before. I have no memory of that flight, so I had to be semi-comatose or heavily sedated.

My theory is that once I was pulled from the burning wreckage, I was placed in a triage situation for evacuation. I believe that I was placed near the wreckage where Bud Traynor came upon me. And the two guys who found me had placed me there for evacuation before walking off to help others. Siddoway said he was escorted to the morgue that next day by two CIA agents wearing flight suits and no name tags. They asked Sid how I was doing because they thought I was not going to make it. They told Sid that they worked with Air America, which we all knew as an arm of the CIA.

Many years passed and all that time, my memory was cloudy about who rescued me and who visited me in the hospital. For a while, I thought that Bud Traynor and Ray Snedegar had rescued me. Finally, after 26 years I was reunited with Ray and was anxious to hear his story. Ray's account made it clear to me that Ray and Bud were not the same two guys who visited me in the hospital. Ray said he saw me crawling toward the wreckage and that I would not stay still. Neither Bud nor Ray remembers visiting me in the hospital at Clark. I spoke to all my surviving crew members and no one could explain exactly how I was rescued.

There were times when I heard crying and screaming in my dreams and occasionally I had nightmares. I would wake up soaking wet. Sad to say, the crash still haunts me to this day. It's hard to get over the loss of so many lives. I thought, why me, why did the Lord save me? For many years I have asked that same question: Why me?

I had just turned 23 years old when the C-5A Galaxy went down and was just coming into my manhood. I've traveled a lot and met a lot of people along the way. Everywhere I've gone, I have touched the lives of many people simply by sharing my story. When I look at it from that perspective it gives me some understanding about why I was saved.

I would often tell the story about how God works through all of us. It doesn't matter how old or young you are, God has a purpose for you in this life. I didn't believe that before the crash, because I was young and figured that I had tomorrow coming. During those days I would have bet money that I would wake up tomorrow and live another day. I was athletic, outgoing, and single; I had no responsibilities, and my life was on track to make something out of myself. The Air Force was good for me; I enjoyed living out of a suitcase. That's what my job required as an Aero Medical Evacuation Technician.

I don't ask that question "Why me?" anymore because waking up every morning allows me to appreciate living. I go to bed with a smile and wake up with a smile. The extra 36 years of life the Lord has given me is a gift.

Somebody had to tell the story about what went on in the cargo section, so why not me? I can attest to what happened and share my account with the deceased's loved ones; maybe help bring closure for family members and friend. I've met DC Johnson's kids, Denise, Harry, Yvonne and Jerry Johnson. I have met Barbara Maier's daughters, Diana Schumacher and Yvonne Shimek. I have met Vicki Curtiss Fernandez, daughter of Dorothy Curtiss. I've met Clara F. Bayot's niece, Yvette Naumu Elliott. All of these people have a very special connection to me and I mourn the losses with them. Each one has thanked me personally for sharing my story. It answered questions and brought a sense of closure for some.

I'm thankful for a second chance at life and saddened by the loss of so many precious souls. I came to those terms after years of soul searching, after years of feeling guilty, and after years of feeling frustrated about why I was saved.

It's often difficult for me to talk about the crash and not get choked up. It took nine years for me to heal emotionally; I finally got to the point where I could talk about the crash. I believe it was because the negativity about the Vietnam War had died down a bit. Vietnam Veterans were not looked down on as much as before. We were called baby killers, hippies, drug addicts -- there was no love for the vets.

Waking up in the intensive care unit at Clark Air Base was truly my second chance at life. I think back to hearing my doctors predict that my injuries would have long-term effects. The injuries to my head, my left eye, my back, my leg, would cause problems including short term memory loss. My attitude was that I will be alright and bounce back. I knew I would overcome my injuries.

I'm still in search of the two guys who saved my life on April 4, 1975. I came close to finding out their identity not so long ago. In 2008, I was the guest speaker at a Saigon Mission Association event in Baltimore, Maryland. I met a gentlemen at the event who had worked for Air America during the time of the C-5A Galaxy crash. He was able to put me in contact with George Petrie, who had worked for General Homer Smith in those days. General Smith had been in charge of the Defense Attaché Office in Saigon and George was his chief liaison officer.

I called George and shared my story with him and asked for his help. George had thought everyone in the cargo section had died, and he was totally surprised to learn of my survival. He said he did an interview in a documentary about the C-5A Galaxy crash and was under the impression that no one survived in the cargo section.

"Yeah George, I saw the documentary," I said. "It's called 'Lost Innocence.' I was shocked that it failed to get it right and that when two of my crew members -- Bud Traynor and Regina Aune – were interviewed, they never mentioned me surviving in the cargo section."

Maybe Bud and Regina did reveal that fact and it was edited out. I don't know, but I thought it was terrible to get the facts wrong. I still hold out hope that someone reading this book may know the two guys who rescued me and can put us in contact. I just want to thank them, give them another big hug and introduce them to my family. I'd like to have them meet my beautiful miracle daughter, who was born after the crash.

George gave me the name of another person to call, Roger Schjedahl. I talked with Roger but he was not able to help me. He focused on the rescue and securing the crash site. I'm grateful to have had an opportunity to meet George Petrie and get his story. George died in 2012, shortly after Major General Homer Smith died. They were true heroes of Operation Babylift. General Smith lost several of his people in crash. Many of the brave women who cared for so many of those kids on the C-5A Galaxy perished. General Smith and Sally Vineyard, who worked in the Defense Attache Office, were instrumental in evacuating thousands of kids and loyal Vietnamese civilians.

CLARK AIR BASE HOSPITAL, 1975

CHAPTER THIRTY

I had the privilege of talking with one of the Air America pilots who helped in the rescue effort that fateful day. Tony Coalson, a helicopter pilot, and his wife were standing near their office building when they saw a cloud of smoke off to a distance. They got the word that the C-5A had crashed. His wife drove to the crash site and Tony jumped in his helicopter and assisted with the rescue. He said flying over the wreckage he didn't believe that anyone had survived. He saw that the flight deck had rolled over to its side and thought that the crew was trapped inside. He went back to the office to get a metal cutter in order to free the crew. By the time he got back the crew members were all out.

Tony began airlifting dead bodies back to the base as his wife assisted with the survivors. The crash field was littered with debris and local villagers were running to the wreckage taking anything of value. They took watches, wallets, rings, aircraft parts, and clothing; in fact one guy took Bud Traynor's flight jacket. Bud said during the rescue he came across a Vietnamese local wearing his jacket. He politely asked for it back and the young man returned it. According to Tony, airplane parts and a lot of debris were taken to a central location. Tony said he did a fly-by near the debris pile to fan the villagers away; but as soon as he turned around to make another bypass they were back again. It took quite a while to rescue the dead; it was just too muddy out there, Tony said.

When I think about those innocent young kids who were on the airplane and how abruptly their lives ended, I wondered many times over what their lives would have been like today. I think about the women who were so gracious and helpful on the airplane. They knew what to do in terms of attending to the kids' needs. I think about their families who did not know what went on downstairs and how their mothers, sisters, aunties, and friends acted heroically in their efforts to save lives. We were caught up in a life and death situation without notice. One minute we were comforting the kids, passengers and patients and the next minute we are looking at the blue sky and clouds.

Today, I feel good about myself and I realize there are no answers other than knowing the good Lord is the Boss. He is the Decider; he decides who stays and who goes on this earth. My advice to all of you is to believe in God; love yourself and family; believe that you have a purpose in life; make the best of your life; help those who have trouble helping themselves; be honest and trustworthy; and don't be anybody's fool, because people who come to you usually want something from you.

It took me some time to understand the effects of this tragedy and how tragedy can strike at any time. It's about what will you do to overcome the trauma, whether it's emotional or physical trauma. Don't give up, talk about it with someone you love and care about or even a stranger. Let the pain escape by talking about it. That's the way I was able to heal. It's not good to keep it in, my friends.

Many people died in the crash and some of their bodies were unrecognizable during the rescue and identification phase. We will never know about all the people who died because we were without a passenger manifest and could not account for everybody on the C-5A Galaxy. My body could have been burned beyond recognition if it hadn't been for the heroes who found me. Was it my white shirt that caught their eyes? Was it spirit that guided them to me, or was I just lucky that day? I don't know, but I have found peace with myself. I don't have to ask why anymore.

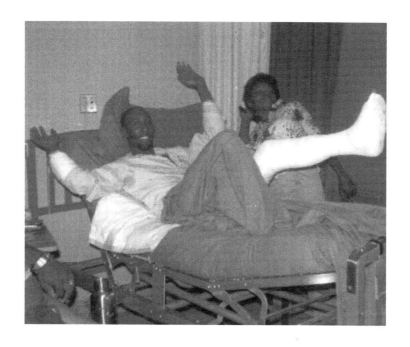

HOSPITAL STAY CLARK AIR BASE, 1975

EPILOGUE

I decided to write this book because the timing is right for me to share a positive Vietnam era veterans story. I wanted to write my book 25 years ago but, America really had had enough of Vietnam stories. America was not feeling the love for the Vietnam era Veterans back then.

America is at war again, but this time it's different: We've won the war in Iraq and are about to wrap things up in Afghanistan. What these men and women are doing to protect our country has inspired me to share my story now.

For many years I'd wondered what the Babylift kids were doing with their lives. I met some of them 25 after the crash. I wanted to know if our efforts to give them a new life had been worth the sacrifice of my lost crew members and the loss of life of the civilian women who volunteered to rescue them. I must say the kids I have met are truly grateful and appreciative for their freedom.

Writing this book is important for me to share with my family because the Babylift experience is what brought us together. I call my daughter (LaNika) my miracle child simply because had I not survived the plane crash she would not be here today.

My boys are my rock in the family. Their names are Ronald and Roderick Amodia, (we call them Bong and Jing). They came to America from the Philippines as little boys and took advantage of what America had to offer. My oldest son, Ronald, served in the US Navy and now is a fashion designer; and my youngest son, Roderick, a college graduate, has retired from the US Air Force.

My boys have given me four beautiful grandchildren (Ronrico, Marquan, Sophia and Lyric) and I love them immensely. When my wife and our two sons first came to America on June 28, 1976, I was a little concerned about moving to Flint Michigan. I knew that Flint would be a tough place for them to adjust to, especially living in an all-black neighborhood. While living in the Philippines I tried to explain the transition that they would undergo adjusting to American life in the "hood." Their English was good but limited and they were only 10 and 8 years old. We placed them in an international academy school where they excelled and quickly improved on their English.

Roderick made a reputation for himself by challenging a neighborhood bully. Roderick and his brother were the only Asian kids living in our neighborhood. We had a paper boy who always teased them when delivering the paper to our house. The paper boy's name was Latrell Sprewell, who grew up to be an NBA superstar. One day Latrell thought he'd pick a fight with my son on the way home from school. What Latrell didn't know was that Roderick had studied martial arts in the Philippines. He soon found out that he was over matched and got his butt kicked while the neighborhood kids looked on. My boys never had any more trouble from anyone else in the hood.

Our boys wanted a little sister and Tessie and I were ready to expand our family. Our daughter LaNika was born July 1, 1979. She was a welcome addition to the family and we all quickly spoiled her. She grew up with the protection of her brothers and everywhere her brothers went, she tagged along.

LaNika went to the Philippines for the first time when she was 2 years old. My wife and the kids went without me that year; and my dear daughter was the talk of the town in the Philippines. My wife's family spoiled LaNika right away, while Bong and Jing paraded her around their barrio proudly introducing her to the rest of her family. LaNika has always been a friendly child and she's just as friendly now as an adult. She is a graduate of Michigan State University and has obtained her master's degree in business management. LaNika models, coaches girls volley ball, and is very active with her church. I'm so proud of my kids and love them dearly.

I would like to express my sincere thanks to my family for their love and support and their belief in me as I wrote this book. Never once did they doubt my ambitions to fulfill my long-time dream of telling my story. They've lived my story. They helped shape the man I am today.

My story is an American story, a story where a young kid took on a big decision when it came to defending our country. I could have gone to Canada. I could have gone to jail. I could have been a conscientious objector, but that wasn't me. Sure, I knew guys that went to Canada or guys who got in trouble just to avoid going to Vietnam. Vietnam was real and the chances of an 18-year-old being drafted were very strong.

I was inspired by men like Johnny Blackmon and James Carr (Marines) and Roy Dukes (Army) who died in Vietnam defending our country. Enlisting in the US Air Force was a good decision for me. I would make the same decision if I had to do it over again. I love my country and the life I've lived.

My good friend Rodney Brown collaborated with me and was very instrumental with editing, organizing and helping me write my story. Rodney is another example of an angel coming into my life at a time when I was seeking guidance to finish my book. His expertise as a documentary film producer made him just the professional I needed to bring my story to completion.

It was truly amazing how we met. We were both guest speakers at the University of Michigan, Flint. Rodney gave a presentation on the Civil War and I gave a presentation on Operation Babylift. I was thoroughly impressed with his knowledge of the Civil War era and the role that black soldiers from Michigan played in winning the war. I sat there listening to his presentation never thinking that he was the person who would play a role in developing my story.

After I gave my presentation we got together and talked, and I told him I was looking a for writer to help with my book. Rodney surprised me and said he was a writer and would take a look at my work. I believe a higher power was at play in bringing us together. We became a team that day and I credit his encouragement to me on writing my own book.

There are many people I'd like to thank as they relate to the Babylift: The C-5A Galaxy pilot, Bud Traynor, and and co-pilot, Tilford Harp, for doing a magnificent job of landing the plane and saving many lives; my crew members who survived the crash and helped in the rescue -- Regina Aune, Marcie Tate, Harriet Neill, Olen Boutwell, James Hadley, Gregory Gmerek, and Ray Snedegar. A special thanks to Susan Derge for sharing her incredible story (below). I'd like to recognize Linda Adams who survived the plane crash and lost her mother, Barbara Adams. Linda and her mom were instructed to go upstairs to help out with the kids. Right before the first impact Linda was positioned between the seats at her mother's request and Barbara was in the aisle. Barbara was killed on the second impact.

My gratitude goes out to Eugene Siddoway and my late friend Dave Harris who evacuated me out of Vietnam. Also, Marcie Wirtz Tate and Harriet Goffinett Neill visited me while I was recovering in the hospital at Clark AFB. They were there almost every day wishing me a speedy recovery. The US Air Force medical team, especially Dr. Kerry Nevins, deserves much credit for my recovery; they fixed me up pretty good.

I'd like to thank my good friends Leon and Sue Jones for their unwavering support and prayers during my recovery at Clark. My good friend Wayne Everingham was there with Sid and Dave bringing me out of Vietnam. Wayne has been there with me through all my battles trying to recover from my injuries.

A special thanks, also, to all my friends and associates at Aero Medical Evacuation Association. The Aerovac association was the first to honor me for the Operation Babylift mission. Much love to my surviving crew member Olen Boutwell and his lovely wife, Lois. Thanks to my best friend Reverend Jim Harden who was right in the mix during the chaos that followed the crash. He volunteered to go to Vietnam to help evacuate the orphans who were trapped at Ton Son Nhut following the crash. I appreciate the prayers that he and good friend Denise Johnke put forth for me. I would like to

175

acknowledge all of the people who I didn't mention that played a part in Operation Babylift's humanitarian mission.

I would like to extend my condolences to Vicki Curtiss Fernandez and her family who lost their mom, Dorothy Curtiss; Yvette Elliott who lost her aunt, Clara Bayot; Yvonne Shimek and Diane Shumacker who lost their mother, Barbara Maier; and the Martini family who lost their mother, Sara Martini.

My late friend Shirley Peck Barnes introduced me to Paul Martini. Paul and I talked over the phone and he wanted to know if his mom suffered during the crash. I could not answer that question, but I described to him what I experienced during those moments when the doors blew off.

Paul had been searching for 30 years for answers about his mother's fate. I told Paul that I had a videotape that one of the crew members sent me. It was the "Lost Innocence" documentary. My crew members Regina Aune and Bud Traynor were featured in it. The documentary had footage of the cargo section before we took off heading to Clark.

I sent the videotape to Paul Martini and to my surprise he called me a week later. He said, "Phil, I'm so grateful to you for sending me that tape! I saw my mom in it. My brother and I watched the tape together and saw our mother." The Martini boys were only toddlers when their mom died. Seeing their mother in the documentary brought closure to them. I felt good about the news and I was happy to be able to help them get through their pain.

Another debt of gratitude goes to Shirley Peck Barnes, the author of the first Babylift book published, entitled "War Cradle." Shirley was the first to encourage me to write my story. She was a tremendous help to me. Shirley once told me, "Phil, this is your story, too, and you should write about it." Unfortunately, Shirley passed in November 2005. She called me right after my knee replacement surgery to wish me well, and she died two weeks later. That was a big loss for me and a greater loss for her family. God bless Dave Barnes and his brother for their loss.

In the summer of 2005, Shirley made it possible for me to travel with World Airway's Homeward Bound reunification flight back to Vietnam to celebrate the 30th anniversary of the World Airways Operation Baby Lift flight. World sponsored the event and carried 20 of the original Babylift kids back to Vietnam that they airlifted out 30 years before. I was a guest of Jared Rehberg, a Babylift adoptee who is a dynamite musician. We met in New Jersey after we did a presentation at the 30th anniversary of Operation Babylift at the New Jersey Vietnam Veterans Memorial Center. It was a great trip to Vietnam and my first time back there since the crash.

World Airways flew re-striped its huge MD-11 jet to the same pattern it had 30 years before to commemorate the historic flight back to Vietnam. Many dignitaries were on board along with a number of special guests including Shirley Barnes and Sister Susan MacDonald. Bud Traynor and his lovely wife, Pam, were there there. Bud was truly surprised to see me on the guest list. In-fact, he said, "Phil, how did you get on this flight?" I kindly answered, "My good friends Shirley Peck Barnes and Lana Noone played a role in getting me on this flight, and thanks to Jared Rehberg, I'm his guest."

I managed to get autographs of all the guests who attended World Airways' Homeward Bound 30th anniversary Operation Babylift trip. It's a souvenir that I will always cherish.

I would like my readers to understand the importance of living your life to its fullest, every single day. Let your loved ones know that you love them on a daily basis, because the old cliché is true, "No one is promised tomorrow." I found that out at the age of 23. Hopefully, what one may take away from this book is that we all have a purpose in life. Young people may not realize it right now, but they do have a purpose in life, too. God works through all of us. There's no age discrimination when it comes to doing God's work. I didn't know what my purpose in life was at the time of the plane crash, but now I do. It's simple: the Lord is real, just spread the word.

What I knew during that time in my life was that I believed in God whole heartedly. I helped the old and looked out for the young and I never did anyone any harm. I've been given a second chance in life. And I have traveled across the country telling my Babylift story, letting folks know that God is real. I'm able to tell my story today because God wasn't ready to take me back then. I've touched the lives of many people by sharing my story. People like the Curtiss sisters, the Maier sisters, the Martini brothers, or the Johnson's siblings and the kids I've met who survived the plane crash. They were too young to remember what went on. Those are the lives I've touched, to name a few. God bless you all and God Bless America.

**PHIL, EMMA, AND SAFI AT CRASH SITE,
2010 REUNION VIETNAM**

**PHIL AT PRESIDENTIAL PALACE WORLD AIRWAYS
HOMEWARD BOUND REUNION, 2005**

**HARRY AND DENISE JOHNSON, PHIL WISE AND
MARCIE WITZ TATE, 2005**

**MY DAUGHTER LA NIKA WISE,
TIA KEEVIL AND PHIL WISE**

ST. LOUIS REUNION, 2011

PHIL WISE, MARCIE WIRTZ TATE, AND HARRIET

**SISTER SUSAN MOTHERLAND TOUR BACK TO
VIETNAM 2006**

CRASH SURVIVORS: JOAKIM KIM KRONQVIST, PHIL WISE, SAFI-THI-KIM DUB, BENOIT THOREL, EMMA MC CRUDDEN, ANNABELLE BOMMELAERE

JIM HARDEN, PHIL WISE, WAYNE EVERINGHAM, MARCIE WIRTZ TATE, JOHN OLESON, DENISE JOHNSON, AND HARRY JOHNSON

REGINA AUNE AND PHIL WISE

MARCIE WIRTZ TATE, OLEN BOUTWELL, PHIL WISE, COLONEL REGINA AUNE, 2006 OPERATION BABYLIFT MEDICAL CREW REUNION IN SAN ANTONIO, TEXAS

PHIL AND BERNIE "DOC" DUFF

DAUGHTER LA NIKA WISE, PHIL AND TESSIE WISE

SUSAN DERGE, SURVIVOR C5-A GALAXY CRASH APRIL 4, 1975 , AND PHIL WISE REUNION IN CHICAGO, JUNE 2012

AFTERWORD

After many years of searching for Susan Derge, a survivor of the troop compartment, I finally found her. I heard about Susan's story when I was in the hospital at Clark AFB. I remember the chatter about a young girl who lost her ear during the C-5A crash and how she helped rescue the kids not knowing her ear was almost torn off. I knew she was in the hospital at the same time I was, but we never met. I was in quarantine when Susan was admitted; therefore our paths never crossed. Until recently I never knew her fascinating and heroic story.

Susan Elizabeth Derge, a civilian survivor, was honored on May 10, 1976, by the Commander of Military Airlift Command, General Paul K. Carlton. Susan also was cited for heroism and was presented a certificate of appreciation by Maj. Gen. Alden Glauch, 21st Air Force Commander.

Susan received a Western Union Telegram from General Carlton that reads: THE EXTRAORDINARY HEROISM WHICH YOU DISPLAYED AT THE TIME OF THE C-5 CRASH NEAR SAIGON ON 4 APRIL 1975 IS TRULY COMMENDABLE. I WAS PARTICULARLY IMPRESSED BY YOUR SELFLESS EFFORTS IN PROVIDING LIFE-SUSTAINING OXYGEN TO THE VIETNAMESE ORPHANS DURING RAPID DECOMPRESSION PREPARING THEM FOR IMPACT AND ADMINISTERING AID TO THE INJURED AFTER THE CRASH. THE FACT THAT SO MANY SURVIVED CAN BE DIRECTLY ATTRIBUTED TO YOUR COURAGE AND PROFESSIONALISM. PLEASE BE ASSURED THAT YOUR HUMANITARIAN ACTIONS ARE DEEPLY APPRECIATED NOT ONLY BY THOSE YOU HELPED TO SAVE BUT ALSO BY ALL MEMBERS OF THE MILITARY AIRLIFT COMMAND.

Susan Elizabeth Derge. Official statement taken on April 10, 1975 by the C-5A Collateral Investigation Officer:

My name is Susan Elizabeth Derge. My address as of yesterday was 204 Pastuer, Saigon, however, my family just left Saigon and I don't know if they will return so I don't know if you can rely on that address. I don't have a stateside address. My father works for Esso Eastern. I am not married. I am 19 years old. I have a younger sister who is 18, older sister who is 24, and an older brother who is 25.

Two months ago when I came to Saigon I fostered a Vietnamese boy who is 2 years old who was to go to a family in Indiana; and I had asked if I could take him to Indiana when it was time for him to go. So, about two hours before the flight left, the head of the orphanage called me and said, "The flight will leave in two hours. You and Bien Hoa (who is the baby), would you please be at the orphanage at that time." The first orphanage we went to was called Friends for All Children. It's referred to in Saigon as New Haven Orphanage and we met there and picked up the infants. I think we picked up about half of the infants (about 20) at the orphanage. These are children maybe under 1 ½ to 2 years old.

We went to a different orphanage at Votan and this was the orphanage that had older children. When the children are old enough to walk, they move to the orphanage at Votan. This flight was supposed to take all the children that had been placed for adoption already. They had assigned parents in the United States. We picked up 20 from the Fondon Fon Orphanage at Votan. I understood that there were another 20 or 30 from another orphanage but there were more than that on the plane. I don't know where all the rest of the others came from. There were several large buses and a few cars. We went out to the airport, with police escort, and straight to the plane. There were quite a few photographers around. I only noticed one Vietnamese newsman. I had one large bag, one small carry-on bag and one shoulder thing. There was pretty short notice to take the baby and get everything packed.

Things were very orderly, when I got to Tan Son Nhut. Everything was well prepared. We waited in the car while they unloaded what looked to be two or three tanks off the plane. On the plane were -- I couldn't say exactly how many -- Vietnamese soldiers and some American soldiers. There were also Vietnamese and American soldiers on the ground around the plane.

After about 15 or 20 minutes, they motioned for us to pull up the loading ramp. They started loading the infants that couldn't walk and they started out doing it by carrying two kids upstairs and then they would proceed up the stairway in the plane to the top. Then they decided that was kind of dumb because people were going both ways on the ladder on the outside of the plane; so they formed an assembly line and handed the babies up one at a time and put the babies in the seats--- two in each seat. Some of the children who were placed on the top were not infants. I was asked to go on top, and I wanted to anyway since my child was on top.

It was sort of a tense situation because the children were all crying. Other than that everything was going quite smoothly. They put the babies about eight or nine to a row upstairs, two in each seat. The only time I went downstairs was to take one child down who would not sit in a seat, and at that time I saw on one side of the plane on the benches a row of American women that I guess were there to take care of the children and on the other side were the row of Vietnamese children.

They had blankets spread out on the floor and some mattresses spread on the floor to put children and infants who would not fit upstairs. They just laid them out on the floor. Some of the women were on the floor with the children. Then I went back upstairs and from then on I have no idea what went on downstairs. Since the children were really jam packed into the seats, we sat on the floor during takeoff.

One Air Force man said, "If you hear a horn lay down on the floor." I heard him say it to a couple of other people. When the plane was getting ready to take off all the children were screaming and we were giving them bottles and milk and that type of thing. We took off. In the beginning we were all going around trying to take care of all the children. Just everybody walking up and down the rows; but after a few more came upstairs, we decided we had enough for each person to have one row of children. So each of us would take care of eight or nine kids. It seemed like a very short time afterwards, I would guess 20 minutes after, I have no idea really of the time, there was a vibration and a very muffled sound. It was simultaneous with the oxygen masks dropping. Everybody dropped to the floor, the Air Force guy in front of me pointed to the masks to all of us.

We pulled the masks down and started them going, pulled them all down and we were sort of alarmed because there were six masks for nine or 10 people along the row. I tried to pass the masks back and forth. I had three older children in my row and the rest were infants; and the infants in my row, I don't want to say passed out, because it isn't as if they were going to faint, but they just became very drowsy and then were all quiet and their eyes were closed. The older children had masks and were passing it to the little children next to them once in a while.

In the beginning when I had the mask on I would take it off once in a while and give it to another child, and I wouldn't really notice any difference. I sort of felt like I didn't need the mask at all but once in a while I'd bring it back to myself anyway just in case. Because if the children were all zonking out I didn't want to do the same thing. Then a man and one of the flight nurse came upstairs, and they both had some kind of insulation material in their hair in very small pieces. At first I thought it was baby diaper cotton that had somehow blown apart. He said we are going back to Saigon and I don't think by this time we were using oxygen masks anymore.

They stayed upstairs, and the flight nurse on the other side of me was very upset because she said the emergency wheels were coming down. And we all just sat down on the ground and were talking to each other and trying to make the kids not panic. There were some blind kids who were upset about flying, let alone everything else that was going on. We were just going down. There were no windows. We had no idea if we were over water or land. A few of us asked if we were over water and everyone said, "No."

We went down and hit very hard. The first time we hit I let go and then the second time we hit I was thrown somewhere. We were all sitting on the floor, squatting. We tried to figure the best way we could position ourselves for a hard landing without injuring ourselves. Most of the children were still strapped in when we landed. That was the first impact.

The second time when everything was really jolted, I'm sure all the lights went out. Someone who was behind me jumped up and ran forward and so I ran forward and grabbed my own child, and the child in the seat next to him. The emergency doors had both collapsed. From the outside the compartment we were in looked like a bunker. It was covered with mud. There was a wing over here, cockpit over there, literally turned over.

You could see the tracks where we came in. You couldn't see the bottom half of the plane anywhere. Everyone was very calm. They got out and at first they started bringing babies out very quickly. Then people began to realize that that part of the plane was in no danger so they decided it would be better if they just let the children stay in until some kind of help came. We didn't know where we were at all. We landed in a marsh which was very uneven. Some people said we were up to our waists. I didn't see any parts of the swamp that went past the knees.

The only form of panic, and you couldn't even call it panic, was someone saying very loudly that we didn't have any radio. They didn't know where we were. Otherwise everyone else was very orderly; in fact, my ear had come off and I went to a gentleman and said, "I'm not panicking so please don't panic when you see this." I think I was in shock otherwise I would have had a fit. And I said, "I think my ear has come off. Would you please put it back on because I don't want to lose it." And so he placed it on and put his handkerchief around there and then I carried two children out and handed them to another girl and lay down on the grass because I couldn't stand anymore.

Then the helicopters came and picked us up, and took us to a South Vietnamese Army Hospital and later took us by ambulance to the Seventh Day Adventist Hospital in Saigon.

I was about one-third of the way back from the front, so there were still two-thirds of rows of seats behind. I was closer to the latrine than to the galley or the ladder stairway. I couldn't even call the noise an explosion because when I heard it I had no idea what it was. I wouldn't describe it as an explosion.

Someone said right after it happened. "It sounds like the door has come out and air has been sucked out." And then I thought that was possible but at the time it never occurred to me that it was an explosion for some reason. It was too muffled. It wasn't loud enough, except that at the same the oxygen masks came down or almost right after and I was more involved with that. I was paying more attention to that than the noise. I did not notice that we were descending. I thought the plane was a lot smaller than it was when I saw it. I didn't realize the size of it. I've been in small planes, where I'm used to moving very shakily and going down very quickly and misjudging the size of the plane I considered it to be normal. The thought of crashing never occurred to me until impact. It never occurred to me at all. Everybody was talking about whether the plane was going to impact and what we should do.

I was looking for the body of the plane after we finally came to a stop and couldn't see it anywhere. The floor of the upper deck was all that was under us. It just looked like a little bunker. It was amazing and the marsh was like, well I didn't really stand there and scale the whole area, but it seemed to me very small area. That pilot did an amazing job of getting that plane down, because there were trees, there were ... it was just amazing the way he landed it and saved as many people as he did.

***

For many years I've searched for answers regarding different accounts of what went on in the troop compartment (upstairs) of the C-5A Galaxy crash. I was excited to reunite with Susan Derge who survived in the troop compartment. I didn't know her on that fateful day of April 4, 1975. Our paths crossed for different reasons back then. She was escorting an adoptee back to the United States, and I was on military assignment. It was rare for me to talk to someone who was not in the military that played a role in the Babylift. Susan's account is another piece of a large puzzle that tells the Babylift story. My hopes are to meet more survivors of the crash as I try to piece together this Babylift puzzle.

The majority of the passengers in the troop compartment were babies, but there were adult civilians helping out there, as well. Those adults have stories to tell about their experiences with surviving the plane crash. Maybe one day our paths will cross. Maybe this puzzle will be completed in my life time. As long as I'm alive I'll be searching for other survivors. Every life is precious and every child's life is fragile. It was America that rescued and delivered these valuable souls to freedom throughout the free world. That's why I'm so proud to be an American and a part of that Fragile Delivery called Operation Babylift. God Bless America!

Acknowledgements:

RODNEY W. BROWN, DIGITAL HISTORIAN, TV PRODUCER
LURMA RACKLEY, EDITOR
SHIRLEY PECK BARNES, AUTHOR OF "WAR CRADLE"
LARRY ENGELMANN AUTHOR, "TEARS BEFORE THE RAIN"
TONY COALMAN, CRASH SITE PHOTOS COURTESY OF TONY COALMAN
LANA NOONE, AUTHOR OF "GLOBAL MOM"
LEANN THIEMAN & CAROL DEY, AUTHORS OF "THIS MUST BE MY BROTHER"
ADAM PERTMAN, AUTHOR OF "ADOPTION NATION"
SUSAN CAROL MCDONALD, AUTHOR OF "FOR CHILDREN CANNOT WAIT"
RONALD AMODIA, COVER DESIGN
SOPHIA KAPRI AMODIA, COVER LAYOUT
BARBARA PARESI, SCREEN PLAY WRITER & PRODUCER
RICK HAMPTON, WRITER, JOURNALIST
MY MOTHER MINNIE ZELL VINCENT
MY FATHER ROOSEVELT WISE JR.
MY LATE SISTER PAMELA WATKINS
MY SISTER FELECIA WALL
MY SISTER JOYCE SEAY
MY BROTHER CEDRIC FREEMAN
MY BROTHER RICKIE WISE
MY BROTHER KERWIN WISE
MY BROTHER DARRELL WISE
DR. KERRY NEVINS
DR. HOWARD F. WEBB AND VA STAFF
DR. MARK DYBALL
DR, ELMAHDI SAEED
COLONEL DENNIS (BUD) TRAYNOR, (PILOT C-5A GALAXY)
COLONEL TILFORD HARP, SURVIVOR, (CO-PILOT C-5A GALAXY)
COLONEL REGINA AUNE
COLONEL MARCIE WIRTZ TATE
HARRIET GOFFINETT NEILL
OLEN BOUTWELL
GREGORY GEMERIK
JAMES HADLEY
SUSAN DERGE
RAY SNEDEGER
REVEREND JIM HARDEN
WAYNE EVERINGHAM
DENISE JOHNKE
CLARENCE JOHNSTONE

Acknowledgements (continued):

CLETUS BELL
PAULINE ISOM
CORNELIUS NICHOLS
CURTIS SMITH
WORLD AIRWAYS
ABC NEWS MAGAZINE 20/20
MICHIGAN LUMBER COMPANY
VIET ORIENT TOURS, NGUYEN HUU VIET
RICK HAMPTON, WRITER, JOURNALIST
LEON JONES
MRS.SUSANNE HENRY JAKEWAY, MY THIRD GRADE TEACHER
BERNIE (DOC) DUFF, ARTIST OF THE PORTRAIT OF PRESIDENT
GERALD R. FORD
BARBARA OLSON TWEED AND FAMILY
RALF VILIET
CRYSTAL FLYNN, UNIVERSITY OF MICHIGAN FLINT
FLINT JOURNAL
DANNY SCHECHTER, PRODUCER
LANIKA R. WISE
RONALD AMODIA
RODERICK AMODIA
ROCHELLE WISE
SYDNEY SEWELL
DR. JOYCE TAYLOR HARDEN
 MAURICE ELLISON
MARY ELLISON
DARIUS WISE AND FAMILY
MARION RICE AND FAMILY
LARRY AND BERNICE DAVIS
CHUCK CHATMAN
JOSH CHATMAN
TERRY CHATMAN
MARLA CHATMAN LANE
JARED REHBERG, MUSICIAN
JIM WILTON
SAFI-THI-KIM DUB
JOAKIM KIM KRONQVIST
BENOIT THOREL
EMMA MC CRUDDEN
MAJOR JANELLE HARDEN JACKSON, USAF, MY BELOVED GOD-
DAUGHTER

Acknowledgements (continued):

JENNIFER NGUYEN NOONE
JANE GOUJON
MAGNUS DOMSTEDT
FELECIA CORCORAN
SARA JOSEFSSON
SHANE DEWEY
JIM ZIMMERLY
CASEY BORGMAN
DANIEL BISCHOFF
LOIS BOUTWELL
SANDY AND CORA THOMAS
TED COLEMAN
JOSE AMODIA AND FAMILY
LIBERATA CAPA AND FAMILY
CIPRIANO DAEL
ROSEMARY TAYLOR
SISTER MARY GAGE NELLES
SALLY VINYARD
BILL DOTY
YVONNE M. SHIMEK
DIANA SCHUMACHER
THELMA WILEY, SURVIVOR, C-5A GALAXY
LIV VILDE ADAMS, SURVIVOR, C-5A GALAXY
CATHERINE THUY-HANG PELLETIER, SURIVIVOR, C-5A GALAXY
MICHELLE AGUILLON
EUGENNE SIDDOWAY
BILL LLOYD
STEVE DAVIS
CYNDI DAVIS
JERRY JOHNSON
DENISE JOHNSON
HARRY JOHNSON
YVONNE PICKERING
FREDDI E. MOODY
DAVE BARNES
VICKI CURTISS FERNANDEZ
YVETTE NAUMU GETTNER
ED GOSSELIN
ANN VERMEIRE
CHERIE VELKOVICH CLARK
ANNABELLE BOMMELAERE

Acknowledgements (continued):

JAMES (JIMMY) WESLEY
DAVID MILLER
PATSY PAYTON
THURSTON (BIRD) JOHNSON
JOHN HIGUERA
WILLIE TURNER AND FAMILY
BILLY FIELDS AND FAMILY
ROGER NEELEY AND FAMILY
DUANE WALKER
VERNEL WILLIAMS AND FAMILY
MIA WILIAMS, (GOD-DAUGHTER)
RENA NILES AND FAMILY
EDNA HUGE AND FAMILY
LATESA PYE AND FAMILY
OTIS WISE AND FAMILY
MENCHU MEDINA
MANUEL MEDINA
MARK SHOSTROM
KIRK GILLON. DOCUMENTARY FILM PRODUCER
MARZELLUS WILSON
STEVE WALL
SUSAN WALL
MARSHALL BROADNAX
ARYN LOCKHART
THE GERALD R. *FORD PRESIDENTIAL* LIBRARY & MUSEUM
MOTT COMMUNITY COLLEGE
ROSS MEADOR
ALLAN TORRES
RUDILIE TORRES
PAUL CROGAN
ROCHELLE CROGAN
NOEL AMODIA
EDO AMODIA
PRAXIE MARIOT
REMA AMODIA MARIOT
ROSS MEADOR
WANDA ZIMMERLY
CANDACE BROWN
TRENTON SMILEY
LEON COLLINS
UNITED STATES AIR FORCE
AND ALL WHO HAVE BELIEVED IN ME OVER THE YEARS

ABOUT THE AUTHOR

Phillip R. Wise is a retired US Air Force veteran and recipient of the Airmen's Medal for heroism. Phillip enjoys touring the country as a speaker sharing the experiences of his diverse life and the humanitarian mission involving the Operation Babylift airplane crash. He has a deep devotion to his family whom he loves immensely. He lives in Flint Michigan with his wife, Tessie, and their dog, Chloe.

For more information go to: www.fragiledelivery.com

Made in the USA
Monee, IL
19 October 2021